As Seen in TechCrunch

The Founder's Guide to Visas & Green Cards

ASK SOPHIE™

SOPHIE ALCORN

Acknowledgements

Thank you to my wonderful family, my amazing legal team at Alcorn Immigration Law, my comprehensive editorial team at Techcrunch, and my dear friends for supporting me in writing this book.

Thank you to my clients, past, present, and future for sharing your journeys with me. You have and always will inspire me.

May all of our endeavors coalesce to support life on this planet we call home - and beyond!

DISCLAIMERS

IMAGE DISCLAIMER:

- *Top Cross-Country Migration Corridors: Ethan Mollick's visualization of data from Miguelez and Fink (2013)*
- *Number of Immigrants and Their Share of the Total U.S. Population, 1850-2021, Courtesy of the Migration Policy Institute (MPI) Data Hub*
- *Images of Kieran White, Xiaoyin Qu, Mandy Feuerbacher.*

TAX ADVICE DISCLAIMER: Any tax information contained in this communication (including attachment(s)) is not intended to be used, and cannot be used, by you for the purpose of (1) avoiding or attempting to avoid any penalty or obligation that may be imposed by any tax authority (including but not limited to the Internal Revenue Service and/or the California Franchise Tax Board), or (2) promoting, marketing, or recommending to another party any transaction or matter addressed herein.

LEGAL ADVICE DISCLAIMER:The information provided in Ask Sophie™ is general information and not legal advice. To receive legal advice about any specific situation, you should consult a lawyer and provide sufficient specific information about your circumstance for the lawyer to provide tailored legal advice. The information provided in Ask Sophie™ cannot be directed to your specific situation. No matter the level of detail provided in any materials from Ask Sophie™, additional facts in your situation may change the pertinent information or recommended course of action.
Information in this eBook may not constitute the most up-to-date legal or other information. This eBook contains links to other third-party websites. Such links are only for the convenience of the reader, user or browser; Ask Sophie™ does not recommend or endorse the contents of the third-party sites. All liability with respect to actions taken or not taken based on the contents of this eBook are hereby expressly disclaimed. The content in this eBook is provided "as-is"; no representations are made that the content is error-free.
Despite any similarity between your situation and a situation described in Ask Sophie™, you should not rely upon this content as legal advice. In addition, any descriptions of other individuals' situations and outcomes should not be considered a prediction of the outcome of your specific legal situation.
Neither the presentation of the information in Ask Sophie™ nor your receipt of the information creates an attorney-client relationship between you and Sophie Alcorn, nor imposes any obligation on Ms. Alcorn or her law firm. No communication sent by you to Ms. Alcorn or her law firm based upon information received in Ask Sophie™ shall establish an attorney-client relationship or an obligation by Ms. Alcorn or her law firm to keep your communication confidential.

ATTORNEY ADVERTISING AND LEGAL DISCLAIMERS: Read Sophie Alcorn, Ask Sophie LLC, and Alcorn Immigration Law, P.C.'s Attorney Advertising & Legal Disclaimers.

This book is educational in nature.

Immigration rules change frequently.

If you need legal advice, please consult with a knowledgeable and experienced immigration attorney:

Thank you!

Table of Contents

Foreword

Human potential is unlimited, yet bound by artifice.

For one reason or another we love drawing imaginary lines on our blue pale dot suspended mid-universe in the ray of a sunbeam and call them countries.

Each country is a set of ideas and values and no other country believes more in the vastness of human potential than the United States of America — the only country started on an idea.

The world's greatest startup.

Founders drive the human race forward, snapping us out of incremental thinking, taking risks with hard work and toiling upwards into the night for the sliver of a chance of making something new, making something important, and occasionally changing the world.

For such an extreme mindset, it's no wonder founders come from extreme backgrounds: immigrants, refugees and outsiders looking to convert the chips on their shoulders to chips of silicon.

Silicon Valley was built by such founders, by immigrants.

I personally have been (as many others) helped during this incredibly exciting, perilous journey by Sophie's genius in recognizing potential where few could see it.

In offering a sure anchor in an ocean of risk and helping steer safely to the shores of invention, Sophie has been providing opportunity, kind words of encouragement, and the courage to continue to founders who one day will move the world forward and upward.

To that I say: more Sophie, more founders, and more America!

Chaitanya Vaidya
Founder
May 29, 2023

Introduction

Local Maxima

Bluejays, hawks, and little brown songbirds flitted in the needles pine trees. The valley spread out below. The cabin's wide-open balcony doors let in the fresh morning breeze.

A moment later, a hummingbird flew in through the doors. It began frantically slamming its beak against the glass of a nearby window. I tried to open the window but it was broken, and I couldn't divert the fragile creature back out through the balcony doors.

Winded, the hummingbird finally perched on the sill. I was winded too, and frantic.

That's when I noticed a towel in the kitchen. I grabbed it and went outside onto the balcony. I used it to block the window that the hummingbird was trying to exit through. Within seconds, it flew out through the open balcony door, squeaking a goodbye. I turned and it was already hovering far away in the pine trees.

We are attracted to the path in front of us, unable to fathom the great potential of what lies at the peripheries. The great unknown.

The hummingbird was obstinate about that closed and broken window, too terrified to retreat deeper into the house and reassess its available paths. But freedom was always there, if the hummingbird was brave enough to risk it.

CHAPTER 1

Welcome, Dear Reader

Nice to meet you!

Hello, dear reader! I'm Sophie.

This book was a labor of love, written on "paper" in 2023 but written in my mind many years before. When I started Alcorn Immigration Law in my Silicon Valley kitchen with a toddler and a preschooler in 2015, I was on the outside, looking in. I could only hope that one day I would get to work with amazing founders like you.

My mission is to transcend borders, expand opportunity, and connect the world. I am honored to have the privilege of helping the world's most talented and brilliant visionaries get visas and green cards to legally live and work in the United States and build their dreams. Every time a client of mine gets approved, I sleep well at night, grateful that I've been able to contribute at least one small thing to support the betterment of humanity.

By way of background, I am the Sophie behind the "Ask Sophie" column in TechCrunch. I'm a Certified Specialist in Immigration and Nationality Law by the State Bar of California, Board of Legal Specialization. You can subscribe to my podcast, Immigration Law for Tech Startups.

How did I get into this? I started working in my dad's immigration law firm in Southern California as a young teen, and my mom is an immigrant from Germany. I studied International Relations at Stanford University, and graduated law school with honors. I love traveling and that moment when I start dreaming in a new language. I've lived in Frankfurt, Florence, Moscow, and Seville.

Like you, I'm a founder. I bootstrapped Alcorn Immigration Law in Silicon Valley and was ecstatic when we were named the top immigration law firm for tech founders and startups. We are thrilled to support clients from top global universities like Stanford, Harvard and MIT, as well as from prestigious accelerators like YCombinator, TechStars, and Draper University. Our thousands of clients have received investment from Sequoia, a16z, Mark Cuban, and more. Their startups have together raised hundreds of millions of dollars, and are collectively worth billions of dollars.

Everybody on my team is mission-driven. For each of us, helping you is personal in some way.

Let's accomplish, together.

The One Thing

As you can hopefully tell by now, immigration is my thing.

What's yours?

And how can I help you reach your goals?

The kinship between my driving purpose and yours has always been there.

I can't wait to help you achieve your dreams.

But, let me warn you now: U.S. immigration isn't for the faint of heart. But you probably knew that already, picking up this book.

Yes, the immigration process in the United States can be time-consuming, dense, and at times, frustrating. But every challenge is an opportunity.

Whether you are at the beginning of your startup journey and you want the liberty to build in peace in the United States, or you already have some international traction and you want to expand your operations here, there are many paths forward for you.

To support that journey, I've put together a workbook PDF with various activities to help you introspect about your ambitions and plot your path forward. You can request your free workbook with your proof of purchase here.

So, take a read and let me know if you have any questions. There are a lot of free resources at the end of this book, and you can always reach my amazing team at hello@alcorn.law.

Halloween in Law School: Justice is Blind

The Basics

If you're ready to go, bookmark this section and feel free to skip it for now. This is a resource for you to turn back to if you need a refresher or a bird's eye view of what we're talking about at any point in this book.

Here we'll cover the basics of the basics: what do you need to know before you get started?

To begin with, there are two primary types of visas in the U.S.: **immigrant visas (a.k.a green cards and Permanent Residence)** and **nonimmigrant visas (a.k.a temporary visas such as student or work visas).** There are several paths to climb the green card mountain: through employment, family, a lottery, humanitarian pathways, investment, and more. Nonimmigrant visas can be simplified by purpose and grouped by factors such as tourism, work, and education.

To figure out which visa or green card you might need, first you need to get clear with yourself on:

1. How long you want to stay in the United States

2. What you want to do while you're here

A lot of my clients start off timid when it comes to articulating their full desires — for fear of jinxing their futures, they hesitate to give voice to the wants of their heart, not only to me but also even to themselves. But reality is malleable, and so anything is possible. The more clear you can become with yourself about your goals, the easier it will be to manifest them.

I often start by asking potential new clients the "magic wand question": "If you could wave a magic wand and have it do anything — doesn't matter if it's possible or not — what would it be?"

I've adapted the magic wand question for immigration:

"If I had a magic wand and could either erase borders or give you some sort of Citizen of the World Passport, so you could go anywhere and do anything, what would you do and why?"

Sometimes, this question is too broad or mind-blowing for my potential new clients to fathom in the moment. So I become more blunt:

"If I could magically fix your immigration issues instantly and you could move on with your life, what would you do next?"

Some people are happy with a few months in the U.S. to simply visit and scope things out. Others want to work here for a few years to make their fortunes and leave. However, some aspiring Americans, even if they have not yet even visited, resonate with the values of freedom, liberty, and the American Dream so strongly that they already know they want to spend the rest of their lives in this country.

Knowing what you want helps us determine your best path forward.

But we also have to keep the idea of "nonimmigrant intent" in mind.

What is immigrant or nonimmigrant intent? When adjudicating visas and green cards, the law requires government decision-makers to determine your intent: are you looking to make the U.S. your home ("immigrant intent") or just come for a little while ("nonimmigrant intent")?

If you only want to stay temporarily, it's your job to prove it. Our laws were written from an American-centric point of view. The U.S. assumes that it is culturally, politically, economically, and legally the center of the world. Therefore, our immigration laws assume that you must want to stay here forever.

However, most types of visas are only for people who intend to come here temporarily. If you want to live in the U.S. long-term, you're usually supposed to apply for a green card right away (immigrant intent), or you need to find a specific visa that permits you to have these plans later on (dual intent). Therefore, it's your burden to prove that you have nonimmigrant intent if your visa requires it. There will be more on that in later chapters.

The following tables are not a comprehensive list of all of the available U.S. visas, but they are the ones that have been most helpful to my startup founder clients over the years. So, here's what we're going to cover:

Nonimmigrant-Intent Visas

You must be able to prove your intention to depart the U.S. in order to qualify:

Status	Type	Chapter
B	Travel	Chapter 3
F	Education	Chapters 2 & 9
H-1B1	Employment	Chapter 9
J	Travel/Education	Chapters 3 & 9
TN	Employment	Chapter 9

Dual-Intent Visas

You can stay for a few years, but it's ok if long-term, you want a green card:

Status	Type	Chapter
E*	Employment	Chapters 4 & 9
H-1B	Employment	Chapters 2, 8, & 9
L	Employment	Chapters 4 & 9
O	Employment	Chapters 2, 4, 8, & 9

*U.K. citizens are also required to demonstrate a U.K. domicile.

Immigrant Visas

A.K.A green cards and Permanent Residence classifications:

Status	Type	Chapter
DV	Diversity Visa Lottery	Chapter 5
EB	Employment-Based	Chapter 6
FB	Family-Based	Chapter 5
IR	Family (Immediate Relative)	Chapter 5
K	Family (Fiance Visa)	Chapter 5

Important Vocabulary

Here are some key terms to know before we dive in. I'll try ("try" is the operative word here) to keep it short and sweet:

- **U.S. Citizenship and Immigration Services**, or USCIS, is an agency of the United States Department of Homeland Security that runs the country's naturalization and immigration services. Before 9/11 this was called the INS. I'll refer to USCIS often, as your attorney will primarily send them your petitions and applications.

- **Department of Homeland Security**, or DHS, is the U.S. federal executive department responsible for immigration public security and overseeing our country's borders. USCIS is part of it, along with Immigration and Customs Enforcement (ICE) and Customs and Border Protection (CBP). In a nutshell, DHS enforces the immigration laws because CBP enforces lawful entry to the U.S., USCIS provides immigration benefits, and ICE arrests and deports immigration violators.

- **Department of State,** also known as DOS or the State Department, is the U.S. federal executive department responsible for the country's foreign policy and relations. All

21

the U.S. embassies and consulates around the world belong to it. Its Bureau of Consular Affairs is responsible for issuing visas. DOS also releases the monthly Visa Bulletin and runs the Diversity Visa lottery (more in Chapter 5).

- **U.S. Embassies and Consulates** are diplomatic offices that are legally considered in the jurisdiction of the country they represent, rather than the country they are geographically in. For the U.S., they are overseen by the State Department. Whereas an ambassador works in the embassy in the capital city, there can be several consulates in satellite locations. Visa interviews can be held in embassies, consulates, and even external offices and processing centers.

- **Premium Processing** makes me very happy, and I hope it makes you happy, too! It stems from capitalism, and it's where you can pay USCIS more for faster service for certain petitions and applications. Although USCIS has been very backlogged for years, and many applications and petitions can take years or decades to process, with Premium Processing you can typically pay an additional $1,500-2,500 to request a decision in 2-6 weeks. It's usually worth it, as it can save you months or years — though it is worth noting that delays still may occur.

- **Green Cards and Visas** are cards and passport foils, legal documents evidencing various rights to enter and remain in the United States under certain conditions. Whereas a visa allows you to stay in the U.S. for a limited duration and specific purpose, a green card grants you lifetime Permanent Residence in the U.S. and a path to citizenship through naturalization. Green cards evidencing your status are currently issued in 10-year increments and can usually be easily extended assuming you're a law-abiding, tax-paying resident.

- **Status** is different from a visa. The purpose of a visa is to evidence your ability to enter the U.S. Showing your visa to your airline or cruise ship allows them to transport you here (and gives them peace of mind that they probably won't have to pay to transport you back home). However, status is something else: status is what you are granted at the port of entry when you're asking to be admitted in the category shown on your visa. Some people can maintain valid status beyond the expiration of their visa. People already inside the U.S. in one nonimmigrant status might choose to apply to extend status, "change status" to another nonimmigrant category (example: F-1 to H-1B), or "adjust status" to Permanent Residence.

- **Single-Entry and Multiple-Entry Visas** are exactly what they sound like! A single-entry visa allows you to enter the United States once while a multiple-entry visa allows you to enter, leave, and re-enter multiple times. For example, a B-1 visa often lasts for ten years and allows you to enter the U.S. as many times as you want, typically for up to six months per stay.

- **Permanent Residence** is a green card, the golden ticket! It evidences somebody's status as a lawful permanent resident (LPR). In times of yore, some green cards never expired (and at one point they were even red or blue, no green in sight.) Today, they're green again and they need to be renewed every 10 years.

- **Conditional Residence** is temporary Permanent Residence and expires after two years. If you're getting your green card based on a recent marriage to a U.S. citizen or EB-5 investment, it's your job to prove to the government a second time that you are really qualified, and then they'll remove the conditions and give you a 10 year green card. Pay attention to your 2-year expiration date as it's the deadline to apply to remove the conditions.

- A **Social Security Number (SSN)** is a unique identifier issued by the U.S. Social Security Administration. You need an SSN to work and U.S. banks use it to establish your credit. The government also uses it to establish your eligibility for Social Security benefits. If you have a SSN, it's easier to open a U.S. bank account. Usually the earliest time to apply is once you have work authorization in the United States.

- **Adjustment of Status** is the process of applying for a green card when you're already in the United States. You bypass the "immigrant visa" application at a consulate and don't need to travel internationally. Eligible people already in the U.S. usually prefer adjustment to consular processing as it's faster and comes with an EAD work permit that allows for multiple streams of income and even self employment. However, sometimes you can get stuck in the U.S. for several months at the beginning of the process while you're waiting for Advance Parole, so postpone your international travel accordingly.

- **Petitions** are filed with USCIS by a petitioner, a U.S. person or company, to seek the admission of a beneficiary, such as a family member or employee. Historically, the U.S. government has relied on Americans' needs for immigrants as the basis for qualification, in contrast to a points-based system such as in Canada or Australia.

- **Applications** are filed by people for themselves to directly request certain benefits, in contrast to petitions, which sponsor others. For example, if you want to adjust your status, change from tourist to student while inside the U.S., or ask for a work permit, these forms are all structured as applications. Thus, you can be both the beneficiary of a petition as well as an applicant at the same time.

- An **Employment Authorization Document** (EAD) is one type of a document that can authorize certain individuals to work in the U.S. It's unnecessary if you have a green card or if you have a nonimmigrant status such as H-1B, L-1B, or O that authorizes you to work under specific conditions incident to your status. Certain EAD categories allow you to be self-employed, whereas others such as F-1 OPT and STEM OPT come with various restrictions.

A complete glossary of immigration terms can be found on USCIS' website, and we'll define much more jargon ahead.

For now, this short list is enough to get you started!

67 Questions To Ask Your Immigration Attorney

Warning: Don't do this yourself!

Even if you never hire my law firm to help you, please know that it's usually very important to work with an immigration lawyer to file any immigration papers for you. They help you choose the right strategy, confirm your eligibility, prepare and file your papers, answer your questions, and guide you along the way.

To help you find the right attorney, I've compiled a list of 67 questions that founders, students, recent grads, and professionals should always ask potential immigration attorneys. Pick the questions that are most relevant to you, and perhaps start a list of your own.

My workbook contains an activity to help you navigate your way through the list of questions. Request your free workbook with your proof of purchase here!

If you don't understand some of the terminology below yet, don't worry. You will soon, and you can return to this section whenever you need:

The Right Attorney

1. Can we discuss my long-term immigration goals?

2. What's the best strategy for me to reach my goals?

3. What are your qualifications?

4. What is your experience supporting clients in similar situations?

O-1 Extraordinary Ability

5. How much experience do you have with O-1s for people in similar fields seeking similar roles?

6. Do I already qualify?

7. If not, how can I become qualified?

8. What are your resources to help me build additional accomplishments?

9. Can we set it up so I can do all the types of work I want?

10. Should my sponsor be a startup or an agent?

11. How much project management support does your team provide?

12. What resources do you provide for the letters of recommendation?

H-1B Specialty Occupation

13. Should I ask my boss to sponsor an H-1B?

14. Can I get an H-1B to work at my startup?

15. What are my odds in the H-1B lottery?

16. How can I get an H-1B without the lottery?

17. What fees is my employer required to cover?

18. Should I jump straight from F-1 to H-1B bypassing OPT?

19. Can I have more than one H-1B job?

20. Should I seek a change of status?

21. Or should I do consular processing?

22. What's Cap Gap?

23. What if my H-1B does not get selected?

24. How many times can I apply for the H-1B lottery?

25. Should I go for a visa interview after my H-1B is approved?

26. After I'm on H-1B, when can my employer sponsor my green card?

27. What are my options after a layoff?

28. How long can I spend in H-1B status?

E-2 Investors and Essential Employees

29. Does my country of citizenship qualify my company for an investor visa?

30. What happens if I have a cofounder?

31. What investment do I need to demonstrate?

32. How can I obtain an E-2 based on VC funding?

33. Can I bring colleagues who share my country of citizenship?

Other Work Visas

34. Are there other work visas that might suit my needs?

35. What's the process for an Australian citizen?

36. What's the process for a Chilean or Singaporean citizen?

37. What's the process for a Canadian or Mexican citizen?

38. What are the consequences of a J-1 for a Fulbright Scholar?

39. Can I get a J-1 to work for a startup as a researcher?

40. How can I work for a company abroad and transfer back after a year?

Green Cards

41. What are the major types of green cards?

42. Which category is best for me?

43. Can and should I apply for the diversity green card lottery?

44. How long will the process take?

45. Can I shorten my wait with my spouse's country of birth?

46. Do I need a family member or employer to sponsor me?

47. Can my startup sponsor me?

48. Can I sponsor myself and self-petition?

49. What's the difference between extraordinary ability and a national interest waiver?

50. Are my credentials currently sufficient?

Fees

51. What are the estimated government filing fees?

52. Can I get Premium Processing?

53. What are your fees?

54. Are they flat fees or hourly?

55. How are RFEs billed?

56. What's the timeline for when you'll file my case?

57. How should I store and organize my immigration documents?

But wait, there's more!

58. What's the likelihood of a Request for Evidence?

59. What can I expect at my visa interview?

60. What can I expect if I'm questioned at the airport?

61. When do I need to pay U.S. taxes?

62. Can I work on the side as a contractor?

63. What should I do if I overstay or violate my status?

64. What if I get charged with a crime?

65. What if I fall in love with an American?

66. How long until I can become a citizen?

67. When can I bring over my parents?

A Brief History of Immigration in the United States

How did we get here? Let's talk about the history of immigration in the U.S. — and where you fit in.

The U.S. is and remains to be, at its very core, a nation of immigrants:

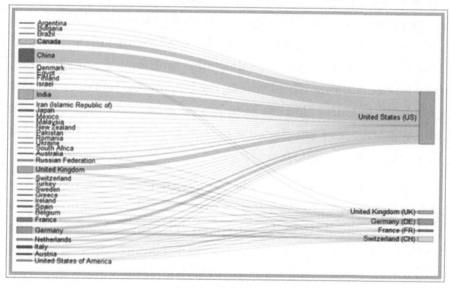

Top Cross-Country Migration Corridors
Ethan Mollick's visualization of data from Miguelez and Fink (2013)

Native Americans lived on the North American continent for thousands of years until European colonization of the Americas began in the late 15th century. North America has received countless waves of immigration over the last 500 years: from religious refugee pilgrims in the early 1600s, to those like you who come seeking new opportunities today.

After centuries of immigration to the continent, the Revolutionary War led to the birth of the United States in 1776, a beacon of hope for billions.

The story of U.S. immigration is also fraught with moments of darkness. By 1790, nearly a million slaves were forcibly brought from the Africas to the U.S. Historically, many people who could not afford passage became indentured servants. Slavery was abolished as a result of the Civil War, but waves of prejudicial immigration laws, like the Chinese Exclusion Act of 1882, continued over the centuries.

In the late 19th and early 20th centuries, nearly twenty million immigrants arrived by ship to Ellis Island in New York, Angel Island in San Francisco, and other ports. Between the years of 1900 and 1915 alone, more immigrants arrived in the U.S. than in the previous four decades combined. After this influx, anti-immigrant legislation proliferated. During World War II, the U.S. imprisoned over 100,000 people of Japanese descent in internment camps, which President Jimmy Carter later concluded was based on racism, and could not be justified by wartime fears.

The foundational law for today's modern immigration system is almost 60 years old. In 1965 the U.S. Congress passed the Immigration and Nationality Act (INA). Although several amendments to the act have been made over the last half century since then, our immigration system still operates under largely the same framework.

Think about it: in our modern world, digital nomads run around with their phones and laptops, jotting off emails and popping into Zoom meetings to get work done anywhere and anytime there's reception. When our immigration laws were originally contemplated, long distance phone calls were prohibitively expensive, and work was often done in offices on typewriters. A tailor who sailed all the way to the West Coast from China to measure his customers for their pants and jackets, and when he sailed home, he had the suits sewn to order, and eventually shipped back to the customers months later.

The INA attempted to be more egalitarian by replacing quotas based on nationality with per-country caps. However, my personal view (with which listeners of the Immigration Law for Tech Startups Podcast will already be familiar) is that the INA created a racist framework because a child born in India or China will not have the same chance to immigrate compared to a child born in Sweden or Japan.

The Immigration and Nationality Act allowed American citizens to sponsor relatives from their home countries, and more. One of the silver linings of our cobbled immigration framework sourcing from various centuries is that it actually provides a variety of legal business immigration routes to the U.S., including even a few options to self-petition for employment-based green cards.

Today, immigrants make up nearly 15% of the U.S. population.

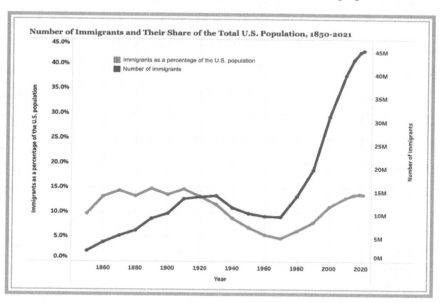

Number of Immigrants and Their Share of the Total U.S. Population, 1850-2021

(Courtesy of the Migration Policy Institute (MPI) Data Hub)

Immigration is a wonderful thing. It brings diversity, vibrancy, and renewed life to our country and culture. According to a report from the Center on Budget and Policy Priorities in 2019, immigrants also bring a multitude of economic benefits to the U.S. They support critical industries; have low rates of unemployment and social service utilization; help support the aging U.S. population, and more.

When it comes to startups, the National Foundation for American Policy found that immigrants have started more than half of America's unicorns, or billion-dollar startup companies — and two-thirds of U.S. unicorns were founded or co-founded by an immigrant or the child of an immigrant.

Thank you, and come in! You are a vital stitch in a complex tapestry that's always being woven.

To start the next stitch in the tapestry, you can always contact my team.

Choose Your Own Adventure

So, what have we learned in this opening section? We covered a few key definitions, and you probably know more about immigration than you did before. As you learn more and more context, I hope that you can more clearly visualize how you're part of America's future.

It's time to take the next step forward. Are you ready?

Use the chart below to help you navigate to the right chapter for your particular situation. And if you have any questions, I'm here to help.

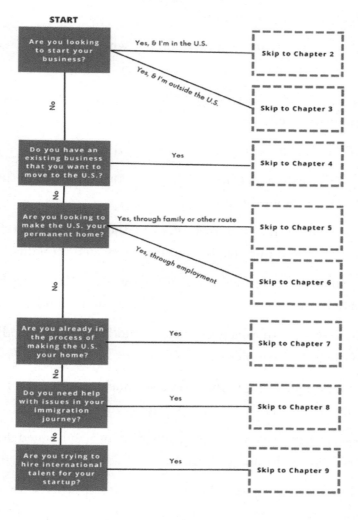

Choose Your Own Adventure

START

Are you looking to start your business?

Yes, & I'm in the U.S. → Skip to Chapter 2

Yes, & I'm outside the U.S. → Skip to Chapter 3

No

Do you have an existing business that you want to move to the U.S.?

Yes → Skip to Chapter 4

No

Are you looking to make the U.S. your permanent home?

Yes, through family or other route → Skip to Chapter 5

Yes, through employment → Skip to Chapter 6

No

Are you already in the process of making the U.S. your home?

Yes → Skip to Chapter 7

No

Do you need help with issues in your immigration journey?

Yes → Skip to Chapter 8

No

Are you trying to hire international talent for your startup?

Yes → Skip to Chapter 9

Creating Your Future

You might hear people talking about manifestation.

We can call it that, or positive intention, or attraction.

We can even call it momentum.

Because when you want something — when you really feel the feeling of having it — things start to change.

After taking a single step you find that the ones that follow are easier, almost inevitable.

Momentum builds, and synchronicities start occuring.

We can call this magnetism or whatever you want, but I'll tell you what I believe about this process.

I believe that we have control over our thoughts. We can choose what to think, and our beliefs stem from repeated thoughts.

And when we decide that we are going to allow ourselves to enjoy feelings of positivity and abundance, more positivity and abundance flow.

The effectiveness of practices such as mindfulness and meditation all demonstrate this potential.

In a process like immigration where so much can often feel out of our control, our mindset is everything.

I have seen the most eminently qualified clients get bogged down by their own negativity and pessimism.

Yet I have also witnessed the magic of easy approvals for people who once didn't have any clue about their own potential, but continually put in the work and did their best to remain open to receiving abundance.

At every moment, we have the choice to think better-feeling thoughts. When we choose to be in the flow, even with life's constant changes and ambiguity, wonderful events can unfold beyond our wildest dreams.

"Forces beyond your control can take away everything
you possess except one thing, your freedom to choose
how you will respond to the situation."
Viktor Frankl

Whether you call this power to choose our thoughts and therefore shape our realities manifestation, attraction, or just plain optimism, keep it top of mind as we work towards your goals together throughout this book.

CHAPTER 2

Starting with the End in Mind: I'm Already in the United States and I Want to Start My Business

Congratulations, dear reader. By identifying your end goal, you've taken the first step towards making it happen. Whether you call it manifestation or simply starting with the end in mind, knowing what you're working towards is powerful. Now let's put that power to good use.

So, you're already in the United States and you want to start a business! You are a founder, and I've helped lots of founders with immigration on the road to building their startups as well as traditional businesses. Let's review your options with the decision tree below.

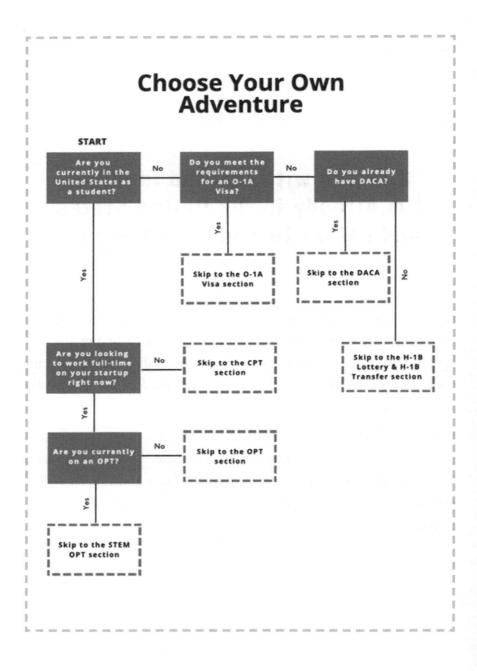

Choose Your Own Adventure

Your Current Status

My clients already in the United States come to my firm as students, J-1 exchange visitors, B-2 tourists, or B-1 visitors. Sometimes as F-1 students they are currently enrolled in school, or they might already have OPT or STEM OPT. Other times we're helping individuals already working for a company such as on H-1B visa. If you are already in the United States and want the right status to start a business such as a startup, this chapter is not exhaustive (you may want to skim through the rest of the book for other options!) but this chapter covers the information that has most typically helped the majority of my clients in your situation.

Changes of Status

If you're already present in the U.S., chances are you have an active visa status and will need to follow a certain process to apply for a different status, which is called a Change of Status. This process will differ compared to applying for one of the visas below while abroad, which is Consular Processing. But essentially, you (or your employer if you're on an employment-sponsored visa) must file a request with USCIS on the appropriate form before your current status expires to extend it, transfer it to a new category, or transfer it to a new employer.

You may apply to change or extend your status if you were lawfully admitted to the U.S., your current status remains valid, you have not violated the conditions of your status, and you have not committed any crimes that would make you ineligible for a new status, and you are eligible for the future status you are requesting.

Until you receive an approval from USCIS, you should assume that you're still on your existing status and act accordingly. For example, you shouldn't start working on your startup if your transfer form an F-1 to an O-1A has not yet been approved! (More on setting up your company and what constitutes "work" below.)

If you're in the U.S., I recommend that you apply for a change of status as soon as you determine it and qualify. Getting a decision can often take twelve months or more, and while the application is pending, you cannot leave the U.S. But as long as your forms have been filed and are currently pending with USCIS, you are not counted as "overstaying" your visa, even if your current status expires. If Premium Processing is available (new categories of applications and petitions are becoming eligible all the time in the Biden administration), I definitely recommend using it!

F-1 Student Visas

The F-1 student visa allows you to study in the U.S. full-time at an accredited educational institution for the duration of your status, which is typically however long the school authorizes on your immigration Form I-20, required for international students.

F-1 Student Visa Eligibility Requirements

To qualify for an F-1 visa, you must be:

- Enrolled in an academic—not a vocational—educational program or a language-training program approved by the Student and Exchange Visitors Program of the Immigration & Customs Enforcement (ICE) that leads to a degree, diploma or certificate

- A full-time student

- Proficient in English or enrolled in English courses

- Able to show sufficient funds to support yourself during the entire period of study.

- Able to show that you have a residence abroad that you have no intention of giving up (see the definition of "nonimmigrant intent" at the beginning of the book).

Note that a student visa requires nonimmigrant intent, meaning that you must intend to depart or change to another nonimmigrant at the end of an F-1. To best position yourself to form your startup in the future, pursue a STEM degree and be aware of the limitations against creating a company while you are on an F-1.

Generally, you can't work during your first academic year (unless your job is on-campus under certain conditions) but after that, you might be able to get up to 12 months of employment through CPT (Curricular Practical Training) or OPT (Optional Practical Training). If you're studying science, technology, engineering, or mathematics, you are also eligible for a 24-month STEM OPT extension after you graduate.

Let's dive in and explore your options.

Curricular Practical Training (CPT)

There are a few key differences between CPT and OPT, the most important being that CPT must be completed before you graduate from your program, while OPT can be completed before ("pre-completion OPT") or after ("post-completion OPT").

CPT is also not available for self-employment. But while you can't start your own company on CPT, you can use this time to conduct research pursuant to the guidelines of your department, or work for an employer. These examples of authorized employment can also eventually contribute toward your O-1A credentials for a post-graduation visa.

The CPT process is free and has a quicker approval turnaround than OPT because it is provided by your campus' designated school official (DSO) rather than the United States Citizenship and Immigration Services (USCIS). You can receive approval within a week in some cases.

You can have more than one CPT authorization before graduation, but you will need a separate CPT authorization for each employer, and you can't exceed the 12-month total for all authorized CPT work.

Important: If you engage in more than 12 months of full-time CPT, you lose your OPT eligibility! However, part-time CPT (20 hours or fewer per week) is not deducted from the 12-month OPT cap. If you want to use STEM OPT, you must apply when you are in regular post-completion OPT.

How to Request CPT

Here are the steps for requesting CPT:

- Make sure you meet the requirements: enroll full-time in an approved academic institution for at least one year, maintain your F-1 status, stay up to date on your tuition, and identify a faculty member who will serve as your CPT supervisor
    - Some universities require you to enroll in a designated CPT course, which may impact your tuition and fees
- Speak to your DSO to find out more about the CPT programs available to your university, the eligibility requirements, and any potential university employers
- Get a job or internship offer
- Submit an I-20 form to your school's internal student office to authorize your CPT. You will be asked to provide the name and email of your DSO as well as the name, address, and dates of your proposed CPT employer
- Once your I-20 has been processed, you will have to apply for a Social Security Number in order to get paid. This can be done at your nearest Social Security Administration card center with the necessary documents

Optional Practice Training (OPT)

Unlike CPT, OPT can be pursued both before (pre-completion) or after you graduate from your program (post-completion) — you also don't need to have a job lined up right away. F-1 students on OPT can accumulate up to 90 days of unemployment before having to leave the United States.

OPT is limited to 12 months. If you have already completed 12 months of full-time pre-completion OPT (40 hours a week), you lose eligibility for post-completion OPT (don't do that!). But let's say you worked part-time during your pre-completion OPT (20 hours a week or fewer) for 12 months: your post-completion OPT would only be reduced by six months, and you would still have six months left of post-completion OPT to take advantage of. From there, you could file your STEM OPT extension.

Good news for founders: you can be self-employed on OPT as long as your work relates to your field of study. Therefore, once an aspiring startup founder receives their EAD (Employment Authorization Document) card, they can start being self-employed or the CEO and majority equity holder of their own startup. They'll want to set up their company and obtain any necessary state or local business licenses to support this.

To apply for an EAD, you will have to prepare and submit your I-765 Employment Authorization Application to USCIS along with any associated documents and the filing fee. The earliest you can apply for OPT is 90 days before your program end date. USCIS now allows for electronic I-765 applications, which makes the adjudication process faster.

Good news: Premium Processing is now available! It's of great benefit, especially if you need to get the card so you can travel internationally. F-1 OPT filers seeking EADs can now file via

USCIS' expedited 30-day Premium Processing for an additional filing fee. Without Premium Processing, it usually takes 3-4 months to find out whether or not your EAD was approved.

While you cannot work before you receive your EAD, I believe that many activities such as forming the legal entity for your company, pitching potential investors, and negotiating contracts should not be considered work because noncitizens are allowed to own companies in the United States. However, many schools advise being on the safe side and waiting until your work authorization is secure prior to incorporating a startup. This is a very fine line. As many related activities, such as coding, conducting research, selling, and creating patentable intellectual property (IP) may all later be considered "work," it's important to consult with an immigration lawyer if you are considering these activities before you have your OPT and EAD.

Once you're on OPT, you will have a full 12 months to focus on operating your startup. Keep in mind: most EADs are valid for one year and it's important to renew your EAD before it expires or change or adjust your status if you want to keep working on your startup in the United States beyond OPT.

STEM Optional Practical Training (STEM OPT)

F-1 graduates with a degree in a STEM field can apply for STEM OPT, a 24-month work permit. You can apply up to 90 days before your OPT EAD is set to expire. E-filing and Premium Processing are available.

If your STEM OPT extension application is filed in a timely manner, but your OPT period expires while the extension is pending, USCIS will automatically extend your employment authorization for 180 days. You are allowed to continue working while it is pending.

STEM OPT has additional requirements compared to Regular OPT. Startup founders must ensure that their employment is properly supervised, which might have implications for the ownership and control of their startup, or for having academic or equity advisors. STEM OPT requires an employer-employee relationship, part time work at minimum wage or higher, a training program approved by a founder's DSO, and their startup's enrollment in the government's e-Verify system.

These steps are all very doable, they just take some planning, time, and a little effort to implement.

STEM OPT Extension Eligibility Requirements

To qualify for a 24-month STEM OPT extension, you must:

- Currently be in OPT status

- Have received a bachelor's, master's or doctoral degree in the field of science, technology, engineering or mathematics from a school certified by the Student and Exchange Visitor Program (SEVP)

- Work for an employer that:
  - Is enrolled and remains in good standing in the E-Verify program
  - Reports material changes to the STEM OPT student's employment to the student's DSO within 5 business days
  - Has a formal training program
  - Provides an OPT opportunity in the student's field of study and commensurate with other U.S. workers in duties, hours, and compensation
  - Completes Form I-983 (Training Plan for STEM OPT Students), which requires an employer to show enough resources and trained workers to train the student, the student will not replace a full- or part-time temporary or permanent U.S. worker, and the work will help the student meet her or his objectives

STEM OPT Extension Application Process

To apply for a 24-month STEM OPT extension, you must:

- Submit completed Form I-983 (Training Plan for STEM OPT Students) to your DSO for their approval

- Ask your educational institution's DSO to sign a new Form I-20 (Certificate of Eligibility for Nonimmigrant Student Status) and update your record in the Student and Exchange Visitor Information System (SEVIS) as authorized for the STEM OPT extension

- Submit Form I-765 and the filing fee to USCIS within 60 days from the date the DSO enters the recommendation for the STEM OPT extension and up to 90 days before your current OPT employment authorization expires

- Submit a copy of your STEM degree and the updated and signed Form I-20 to USCIS

- Submit your employer's name as listed in E-Verify and the employer's E-Verify company identification number or a valid E-Verify client company identification number

- Demonstrate the employer has enough resources and trained workers to train the student, the student will not replace a full- or part-time temporary or permanent U.S. worker, and the work will help the student meet her or his objectives

H-1B Lottery & Transfer

If you founded a startup under OPT, or if you had an H-1B sponsored by another company, your startup could sponsor you for the H-1B lottery in the annual March lottery. This can be frustrating because demand in recent years has been high, meaning that the chances of getting selected are low. For a startup H-1B, it's especially important to work with an experienced immigration lawyer and corporate lawyer to ensure your company complies with the requirements.

How to Structure Your Company

Here are some typical best practices on how to structure your company to best support your H-1B visa process (remember, every company and situation is different, so talk to your immigration counsel!):

- Things are usually simpler if you own less than 50% of your company

- Someone else must formally hire you, supervise you and your work, and have the ability to fire you*

- Your startup has the ability to pay you the prevailing wage based on your position and geographical location as well as cover the company's operations for the term of the visa petition (usually up to three years for an H-1B transfer)

- Generally, U.S. investors want to deal with Delaware C corporations, so consider incorporating there are registering in any states where you have employees or do business

- Get your FEIN number, bank account, physical office space (an office is better than a hot desk), and register your company online in the Dunn & Bradstreet database to minimize the chances for a Request for Evidence (RFE)

*At the time of writing DHS announced that it's aiming to issue a proposal in October 2023 to revise the requirements for employer-employee relationships. The goal is more flexibility for founders!

If your H-1B employer is an institution of higher education, a nonprofit entity affiliated with an institution of higher learning, or a nonprofit or government research organization, you don't have to go through the lottery to get an H-1B because they are exempt. Therefore, they can submit your H-1B any time of year.

You can pair the cap-exempt opportunity with the ability to have two or more concurrent roles on H-1B: If you have an H-1B to work for an exempt employer, you can qualify for a second, concurrent exempt H-1B to work at another company that wouldn't otherwise qualify as cap-exempt. This is the path to work for a normal private company even if you didn't get selected in the lottery.

The demand for H-1B visas consistently outstrips the annual random lottery "cap" of 85,000. If you want to go this route, your startup should be prepared to put you in the lottery every year before you graduate as well as when you're on Regular OPT and STEM OPT, as well as prepare for visa alternatives if you're not selected in the lottery.

Keep in mind: if you're on an H-1B visa sponsored by another company, you are only allowed to work for that company. If you work for your own startup — even without pay — before transferring your H-1B, you risk losing your status and your ability to remain in the United States, and your IP is in jeopardy as it might be the property of your employer.

With the legal advice of an immigration attorney and corporate attorney, there is often a way to legally navigate the following while on H-1B for another employer:

- Create and register an LLC or C-Corp
- Be a passive investor
- Be a shareholder of a company without providing any labor or advisory services
- Volunteer on a startup's advisory board or board of directors without receiving any equity or consulting fees
- Negotiate with future investors
- Meet with board members

Talk to your attorney about any specific activities you want to pursue to determine if and how they are allowed.

Lastly, note that the H-1B visa typically allows a maximum stay in the U.S. of six years. The maximum does not reset through an H-1B transfer alone. Under the American Competitiveness in the 21st Century Act (AC21), your employer can extend your H-1Bs beyond six-years if you:

- Applied for a PERM labor certification 365 days before reaching 6-years of H-1B status

- Filed an I-140 employment-based (EB) immigrant petition more than 365 days ago

- Have an approved I-140 petition but your Priority Date isn't yet current on the Visa Bulletin

These AC21 extensions can help you extend your H-1B in 1- or 3-year increments beyond the normal 6-year maximum. If you were born in India or China, make sure you talk to your attorney about the right green card process for you and starting it on time.

The H-1B is a "dual-intent" status: you are allowed to be here temporarily and it's also ok if you want to apply for a green card. Your startup's ability to sponsor you for a green card with the PERM process can be limited if you hold too much equity, so you should also check your eligibility for the EB-1A extraordinary ability and EB-2 NIW (National Interest Waiver) green cards (lots more on that in Chapter 6.)

O-1A Visa

Instead of the randomness and restriction of the H-1B, I often recommend that early-stage founders invest their limited time, energy, and funds into qualifying and applying for the O-1A extraordinary ability visa. It's much easier to be the CEO and hold equity on an O-1A, there is no minimum wage, you can set up your O-1A to allow you to engage in multiple work gigs, and it's a great stepping stone if you are from India or China and need to get qualified for an EB-1A green card for extraordinary ability.

Even students can apply for O-1s. Although it can take a while to build up a suitable portfolio of accomplishments in your field, an intentional and highly-motivated F-1 student can establish the requisite portfolio of accomplishments through volunteer engagements that do not constitute work, even prior to graduation. I've seen it happen many a time!

For the founder who does not yet qualify for an O-1 at graduation, the period of OPT and STEM OPT (or sometimes even just that initial year) can be ample time to not only found your startup but build sufficient accomplishments to qualify.

O-1A Visa Eligibility Requirements

If you don't have a Nobel Prize (no biggie!), you must meet at least three of the following eight requirements in order to be eligible for an O-1A visa in science or business as a founder:

- Receive nationally or internationally recognized awards for excellence in your field — venture capital funding counts!

- Have articles about you or your startup published in major trade or media publications; often it's "the more the better," but a couple of biggies can suffice

- Write and publish articles for major media or professional publications yourself. Aim for five or more. My editor at TechCrunch is always interested in publishing "how I did this" articles written by founders.

- Judge the work of others, such as serving as a judge at a hackathon or pitch competition

- Accept an invitation to join a group or association that demands outstanding achievements, like a startup incubator or an elite professional association such as a scientific standards committee

- Demonstrate significant contributions to your field, such as disruptive technology, patents (patent-pending now counts!) or peer-reviewed publications

- Receive higher-than-average salary or demonstrate valuable compensation in the form of startup equity

- Prove that you have been a critical or essential employee for a company with a distinguished reputation such as your startup or even a prior employer

Although USCIS only requires applicants to meet three of the eight requirements above, I recommend aiming for four or more to present a strong case.

There's reason to be optimistic! I typically find that early-stage startup founders can get an O-1A in a few months with a little focused effort, if they don't qualify yet. At Alcorn, we provide a complimentary O-1A assessment for founders. An O-1A visa can also put you in a great position to pursue an EB-1A or EB-2 NIW green card down the line.

If you are feeling shy about proving your accomplishments, or don't think you "deserve" this type of visa — suspend your self-consciousness for a while. As a founder, you have to be able to think laterally. I know you can do this, and you never know what amazing fruits will be borne through the seeds you plant through this process!

O-1A Case Study: Kieran White

In my line of work, I am lucky to get to work with hundreds of inspiring, determined founders every year. One of those founders was Kieran White, co-founder and CEO of Return Protocol, a climate technology company that provides consumers, businesses and communities with verifiable and incentivized social climate action.

Kieran wanted to move from the U.K. to the U.S. to join his co-founder, who was a U.S. citizen. Building his startup in San Francisco was always the goal.

When I interviewed Kieran on my podcast, he said: "I read Steve Jobs' biography when I was 15 and since then I've basically been like, okay, I must live in Silicon Valley... I'm just super biased towards the bay area. There's magic there. And there's also the climate angle. They're totally obsessed with climate there... I think this is an amazing place for the zero-to-one creation phase of a business."

Kieran and I met when I spoke to an accelerator. Even though Kieran's startup had successfully raised millions of dollars, the process of coming to the U.S. was anything but easy. They had tried every route in the book — from an L-1A to an L-1B to an ESTA. His immigration journey was a years-long process that involved multiple failed attempts, rejections, and withdrawn petitions.

The frustration was destabilizing Kieran and his founding team. Going back and forth all the time, scheduling meetings across time zones, and navigating the frustrations of the immigration system caused a lot of stress and it was sapping their time, energy, and attention away from actually building.

Kieran described how this process taught him patience. "It will work out. That day that feels like it's never-ending and everything is falling down — it probably will all fall down, but then it'll seem easier than you think to put it back up again. Have faith in the process and be persistent, as if you already know what's going to happen one way or another and you're just playing with puzzle pieces to figure out how and when the details will fall into place."

When Kieran came to me, we examined all the possibilities to support him to have a strong immigration foundation. Kieran wanted to apply for an O-1A, but he wasn't qualified yet.

He enrolled in my online class, now called Alcorn Academy: Extraordinary Ability Prep Course and spent about 18 months establishing his credentials in his field to have as strong of an O-1A as possible.(I've seen it done in six to twelve weeks as well!

Part of Kieran's time was spent trying to get himself and his company featured in as many podcasts and publications as possible. "[The O-1A] is basically a personal branding marketing plan."

Racking up O-1A accomplishments can feel distracting if you're building your startup's MVP, but it's excellent if you're trying to get traction or fundraise. Either way, if you need an O-1, you have to go through the steps of becoming qualified.

I know that the fuzziness of whether you have achieved enough to qualify for an O-1A or not can be frustrating. Engineers trained in deterministic thinking ("Will the bridge fall down?") can be their own worst enemies, afraid to try any of these big and scary things. ("Why should I bother to get interviews if I can code something over the weekend that will get a million users?") This feeling is one of the reasons why it pays off to work with an experienced immigration law team of attorneys and paralegals well-versed in founder immigration: they will hold you accountable and motivate you to get things done in a way that suits your style and helps you achieve your goals. An experienced lawyer's well-honed intuition allows them to tell you when enough is enough and you're ready to file, even if it's not apparent to you.

The benefits to getting qualified for an O-1 extend even beyond immigration, however. I can personally attest that the eight O-1 criteria provide an amazing marketing plan. When I started Alcorn Immigration Law, I was dealing with imposter syndrome. I wanted to help brilliant founders like you, but I felt like I had to prove myself worthy. I followed the O-1A requirements as a roadmap to establishing my firm's credibility. These efforts paid off: my small team gets to help the world's most brilliant people make a difference, I get to write for TechCrunch every week, and you are now reading this book!

I take inspiration from founders like Kieran, and he shared that his curiosity and passion got him through the challenges of immigration journey:

"I will be honest, I was expecting it to be a lot easier... but the thing that differentiates people is that they actually just love [their job], and they would do it anyway, so of course they're going to do it. How can you not love going to work every day and learning ten new things you didn't know existed the day before? Best job ever."

I'm happy to say that ultimately, Kieran's O-1A was approved and he is officially an "alien of extraordinary ability."

Deferred Action for Childhood Arrivals (DACA)

Dreamers are integral to the U.S. and the startup scene is no exception. Created by the Obama administration through an executive order in 2012, the Deferred Action for Childhood Arrivals (DACA) program provides protection to undocumented individuals from deportation and prosecution for being in the United States without a visa or green card.

You might qualify for DACA if you:

- Came to the U.S. before you turned 16
- Were under the age of 31 on June 15th, 2012
- Have lived in the United States since June 15th, 2007
- Were physically present in the United States on June 15th, 2012
- Had no lawful status in the United States on June 15th, 2012, including any active valid visa, green card, or refugee parole.
- Were physically present in the United States at the time of making your request for DACA
- Are currently in school, have graduated or obtained a high school completion certificate or a General Education Development (GED) certificate, or are an honorably discharged veteran
- Have never been convicted of a felony, a significant misdemeanor, or three or more misdemeanors
- Do not pose a threat to national security or public safety

DACA is valid for two years, after which you can apply for a two-year extension. With DACA, you can apply for work permits or Permanent Residence and even start your business.

In some circumstances, you can also receive Advance Parole to travel outside of the United States. The benefit of reentering the United States following international travel with Advance Parole is that your return is considered being "admitted" to the U.S. which can open up the possibility of applying for adjustment of status such as based on a marriage to a U.S. citizen or potentially employment-based categories as well.

USCIS typically grants Advance Parole for three types of travel; its availability is subject to the current state of DACA litigation:

- Educational travel, such as academic research or semester-long study abroad program

- Employment travel, such as overseas projects, conferences, training, interviews, or meetings with clients

- Humanitarian travel, such as to receive medical treatment, visit an ailing relative, or attend the funeral of a family member.

Keep in mind that USCIS usually takes multiple months to process travel document applications. Based on my experience, employment-based Advance Parole is the most difficult to get approved, and humanitarian travel is the most successful route.

How to Apply for DACA

To apply for DACA, you must ensure your eligibility.

I recommend working with an immigration lawyer to:

- Fill out the current version of Form 1-821D (Consideration of Deferred Action for Childhood Arrivals)

- Fill out Form 1-765 (Application for Employment Authorization) and Form 1-765 Worksheet

- Send the forms with the appropriate filing fees and evidence to the designed USCIS location based on where you live and the carrier you use to send your renewal packet

Putting It All Together

We've covered a lot of ground in this chapter, from F-1 student visa options like CPT, OPT, and STEM OPT to other ways to start your business in the United States with an H-1B, O-1A, or DACA. Here's a chart to help you synthesize everything we've learned:

Status	Length of Stay	Approximate Processing Time*	Is Premium Processing Available?	Can I Be a Founder?
CPT	12 months	2 weeks	No	No
Pre Completion OPT	<12 months	1-2 months	Yes	Yes
Post Completion OPT	12 months	1-2 months	Yes	Yes
STEM OPT	24 months	1-2 months	Yes	Yes, with caveats
H-1B	6 years	2-3 months	Yes	Yes, with caveats
O-1A	3 years, with unlimited 1-year extensions	1-2 months	Yes	Yes, with caveats
DACA	2 years, with one 2-year extension	2-3 months	No	Yes

*Processing time here and in all subsequent tables refers to government decision-making time, i.e. from the time of filing until you hear a final decision. These change frequently. Find current rates at USCIS's Case Processing Times.

Ready to sort out your immigration and start your business? Learn more.

On Moving Forward

Are you overwhelmed?

It's not you — the information in this chapter is genuinely complicated. There are a lot of options, requirements, and criteria to keep in mind, not to mention the paperwork, due diligence, and waiting time baked into the immigration process. But you can do it. In fact, you are already on your way.

Just by reading this chapter, you've taken the first step.

Even when it's dark, we can often find guiding lights on the path: this book, the people who care about you and who help you hold yourself accountable to your dreams.

Other times, stars light the way, or our hearts' light provides the only beacon.

The darkest light is just before the dawn. You might not know how far you have left to go, but it doesn't matter.

You just need to take the next step.

Close your eyes and take a deep breath.

It may feel like our paths circle back to where we started, but we are never the same. Even if it's a spiral, we are always moving forward.

And remember: any time we don't get what we want, we get experience.

Keep going, you're closer than you've ever been.

CHAPTER 3

Starting with the End in Mind:
I Want to Get to the United States
to Start My Business

You're not in the United States now, but you see a future for yourself there.

First of all, on behalf of America, thank you. May your inventions and innovations not only positively affect the U.S., but also the world. We need you to create what's in your heart, and you need an environment of peace and freedom in which you can prosper. We're delighted you want to join us, and we're appreciative of the technologies, products, services, and jobs you'll be creating.

You may be interested in participating in one of our startup accelerators and incubators, as well as networking in startup hubs such as Silicon Valley and San Francisco, New York, Austin, and Miami.

These are exciting and worthwhile goals — and fortunately, they're attainable!

In this chapter, we're going to examine how you can achieve your personal and business dreams by coming to the U.S. one day to grow your business.

Let's get started.

Choose Your Own Adventure

START

Is your home country eligible for the Visa Waiver Program?

Yes → Skip to the ESTA section

No ↓

Do you want to come to the U.S. to explore business prospects?

Yes → Skip to the B-1 & B-2 Visitor section

No ↓

Need a way to spend 1+ years learning about the U.S.?

Yes → Skip to the J-1 Visa section

Applying for a Visa

Last chapter, we spoke briefly about the change of status process if you're on a valid status in the U.S. and want to be in a different temporary status. Similar substantive requirements govern the alternative process of applying for a visa while you're abroad. You also can't travel outside the U.S. while a change of status is pending, but you might be able to visit if you are waiting for your petition to be decided and you're seeking consular processing.

If you are applying for a visa abroad, you will likely be applying at a U.S. consulate or embassy. From our definitions in Chapter 1 we know that embassies and consulates are diplomatic offices abroad — embassies are the primary offices and are usually located in capital cities, while consulates are additional offices outside the capital. Either can potentially adjudicate your visa application, depending on your countries of citizenship and residence.

If you are inside the United States, the benefit of consular processing and going for a "visa stamping appointment" is that if you obtain a multiple entry visa, you will have permission to travel in and out of the U.S. freely. If you're outside the United States, you need to go through the consular visa process to get your visa to come and go.

Around the time of publication in Q3 2023, the State Department has been waiving interviews for many types of work visas at various consulates and embassies, decreasing the wait time to get a visa. Additionally, there is talk of a pilot program in late 2023 that will allow certain H and L visa holders presenting in the United States to accomplish their "visa stamping" stateside without the need for travel outside.

For the latest immigration updates, you can always subscribe to the Alcorn Immigration Law newsletter as well as the Immigration Law for Tech Startups podcast.

B Visitors

People from most any country (with a few exceptions where there are no diplomatic ties such as North Korea) can apply for a B-1 business visitor visa, B-2 tourist visa, or B-1/B-2 combined visitor visa to come to the United States as visitors for meetings or pleasure. There are rare exceptions, like citizens of North Korea, with which the U.S. has no formal diplomatic ties. However, even people from Bhutan, Iran, Syria, and Palestine have the legal ability to apply for visas.

To qualify for visitor status, you must demonstrate nonimmigrant intent: that you intend to depart the United States prior to the end of your authorized stay.

There are slight differences between these two categories: the B-1 visa covers business trips while the B-2 visa mostly covers tourism. Usually the U.S. Consulates issue multiple-entry B1/2 visas that are valid up to ten years. When you travel to the U.S. and present this visa for entry, you can be admitted for up to six months (180 days) at a time. Often your admission stamp will reflect both: B-1/B-2 status, which means that either business or pleasure activities are permitted on your visit, but sometimes you will be admitted in only B-1 or B-2 status.

Pay attention to the details of the visa foil placed in your passport by the State Department, as well as the I-94 entry stamp you receive at the time of admission from Customs and Border Protection of the Department of Homeland Security. Access the government's electronic portal to confirm that any dates added to your passport are consistent with the database. Correct any admission discrepancies immediately and consult your immigration attorney if you need assistance.

After You Arrive

In general, you cannot work in the U.S. without work authorization, including while you are in B-1 or B-2 status. However, many business-related activities are not considered employment, and they are permissible while you are visiting in B-1 status. Examples include negotiating contracts, meeting customers, conducting research, consulting with business associates, attending conferences, and participating in trade shows and conventions.

You certainly cannot get individually paid by a U.S. company for activities on your trip. You can, however, conduct the visit on behalf of a foreign company that employs you. If you're unsure about what is and isn't allowed on your B-1 visa, it always makes sense to consult an immigration lawyer.

So while you can't formally enroll in any university studies or accept employment from a U.S. company, you can work on setting the foundation for bringing your business to the U.S. You can certainly meet with investors or do non-work activities to build your credentials toward a future work visa such as an O-1A.

B visas typically allow for multiple entries to the U.S., so you can leave and return while on a B-1 or B-2. The government filing fee for these visas is $185 as of 2023, but keep in mind that this is subject to change and this doesn't include the cost of gathering your documents and evidence and acquiring your passport if needed. The average wait time once you file can vary; during COVID, this time increased to years in many consulates, but typically when the State Department is current with processing, it takes about two months. Make sure to start your application well in advance of your intended travel.

Once your six months are about to expire, if you are in the U.S. and you need to stay longer, you can apply to extend your B status in six-month increments by submitting Form I-539 on paper or electronically. It is available on USCIS' website and you may hire an attorney to help you. Processing times can take much longer than the six months you are able to request, and there is currently no

Premium Processing option. Navigate these extensions carefully and consult with an attorney, because if you stay longer than authorized, you may be barred from returning to the U.S. in the future.

Sometimes people admitted on B-1/B-2 end up deciding, after they have arrived, that they want to apply for a green card (we'll talk more about that in Chapter 5 and Chapter 6). It's important to remember that obtaining the visa and being admitted to the U.S. are dependent on demonstrating good faith nonimmigrant intent. If you find yourself in the U.S. in B-1/B-2 status and circumstances have changed since your arrival and you now need to obtain a green card, talk to an attorney experienced in adjustments of status.

When your visa is expiring, you can apply to renew it from your home country.

How to Apply for a B-1 or B-2 Visa

Want to come to the U.S. for business travel on a B visa? Follow the instructions below:

- Gather the required documents, including:
  - Valid passport
  - Recent digital photograph
  - Documentation of your past five trips to the U.S.
  - Proof of funds to cover the cost of your entire trip
  - Proof of binding ties to your home country (like a job, property ownership, savings or family)
  - Potentially more depending on your circumstances
- Complete Form DS-160 (Online Nonimmigrant Application) online and print out the confirmation page
- Attend your visa interview when scheduled

ESTA: The Visa Waiver Program

The Visa Waiver Program (VWP) allows citizens of many countries to travel to the U.S. for up to 90 days without a visa such as a B-1/B-2. If you live in one of the countries below, you can apply to visit via Electronic System for Travel Authorization (ESTA) rather than a B-1/B-2 visa, and you can pursue all of the unpaid, business-related activities that you normally would under a B-1 visa in order to help set up your business.

You'll need an e-passport to take advantage of the VWP. This is a secure passport with an embedded electronic chip that can be scanned at the airport. If you're not sure if your passport is an e-passport or not, look for a symbol like the one below from the Department of Homeland Security. The process to apply for an e-passport varies by country, so make sure to check with your home country's embassy if you have any questions.

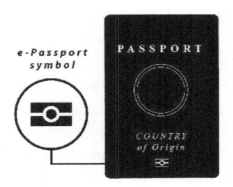

Aside from having a valid e-passport, you have to be a citizen of one of the 40 eligible VWP countries in order to qualify for ESTA. It doesn't matter where you were born or currently live, as long as you are a citizen of an eligible country today. Here is complete list of eligible countries of citizenship as of 2023:

Andorra	Finland	Latvia	Portugal
Australia	France	Liechtenstein	San Marino
Austria	Germany	Lithuania	Singapore
Belgium	Greece	Luxembourg	Slovakia
Brunei	Hungary	Malta	Slovenia
Chile	Iceland	Monaco	Spain
Croatia	Ireland	Netherlands	Sweden
Czech Republic	Italy	New Zealand	Switzerland
Denmark	Japan	Norway	Taiwan
Estonia	Korea	Poland	United Kingdom

Once you enter the U.S. on an ESTA, you'll be given either a WB (waiver-business) or WT (waiver-tourist) in your I-94 record. These statuses align with the B-1 and B-2 visa restrictions in the previous section. You can "Get Your Most Recent I-94" at the CPB's official website to double check it anytime.

Most of the time, ESTA authorizations are valid for two years, meaning that you can visit the U.S. multiple times for up to 90 days each on each visit during that two-year period. There is no bright-line rule about how many days you need to be gone between trips, or how many days you can be in the U.S. in a specific year. If it is true that time spent in the U.S. can be a proxy for your nonimmigrant intent, it seems that usually spending less than half of your 90 days in the U.S. seems to lead to getting admitted on the next visit. There may be other reasons to limit your overall time in the United States such as for tax reasons, for which you would need to consult with your cross-border tax certified professional accountant familiar with the tax laws of both the United States and your home country.

Although your ESTA authorization is valid for two years, you will have to get a new ESTA if you change your passport, name, gender, country of citizenship, or you otherwise need to change any of the responses on your original ESTA application.

Compared to B visas, you can apply for ESTA online more easily and no visa interview is required, but an ESTA only permits you to come to the U.S. for 90 days on a single trip, and you are usually not allowed to change or adjust status after you enter. If you plan on staying longer on a single trip, the B-1 or B-2 visa will likely still be the best option for you. As you can't extend your stay or change your status while on ESTA, you will have to depart the U.S. on or before the 90-day date listed on your admission stamp.

J-1 Visa

The J-1 visa is an educational and cultural exchange visa available to foreign nationals who participate in an approved program for teaching, lecturing, studying, conducting research, consulting, or receiving training or medical education. The purpose of the J-1 is to promote knowledge and cultural exchange between the U.S. and other countries for work and education. It's an attractive option for both participants and employers as there is no cap or lottery for this type of visa.

You can qualify for the J-1 visa with a variety of different backgrounds (anyone from au pairs to camp counselors, government workers to teachers can meet the requirements). You can also bring your spouse and children (under 21 and unmarried) to the U.S. with you, and your spouse can receive work authorization (EAD) under a J-2 visa. Sometimes one spouse may want to obtain a J-1 to work in a specific program, and the other spouse uses the employment authorization of their J-2 status to explore founding a startup.

If you want to learn more about U.S. culture and working here, a J-1 for a limited period to work here might be a good option.

You would need to find a job offer and a sponsor, and you cannot be self-employed. The two most popular J-1s my clients in the startup ecosystem include the 18-month training program and the researcher J-1, which is valid up to 5 years. Private companies are allowed to work with certified J-1 host organizations in order to sponsor you. Keep in mind that this is a nonimmigrant status and if you decide you want to stay longer in the U.S. later, you really ought to pursue that through a new visa obtained at the Consulate.

If you receive an offer for a J-1 role and you notice that your Form DS-2019 or visa foil in your passport says you are "Subject to 212(e)" which is the 2-year foreign residence requirement, think twice about entering the U.S. on your visa, which would activate this requirement. If you come to the U.S. on this visa, you will be required to spend two years in your home country in order to be eligible for certain visas like the H-1B or green cards. Some people who are subject to 212(e) can obtain a waiver of this two-year foreign residency requirement, but many cannot. For example, if you accept a Fulbright Scholarship in the U.S., you will likely never be able to obtain a waiver, unless a very extreme situation arises.

Although the J-1 is a fabulous way to explore the U.S., it's not a fabulous way to become a founder. So, if you already know you want to form a startup in the U.S., you should consider a different route. You can read more about J-1 visas in Chapter 9.

How to Apply for a J-1 Visa

Follow these steps to apply for a J- Visa:

- Find a U.S. sponsor organization to support your application. There are thousands of such organizations across the country that you can connect with online
- Be able to prove that you have a residence in your home country and are able to finance your entire trip, including medical coverage
- Receive Form DS-2019 (Certificate of Eligibility for Exchange Visitor Status) from your sponsor and submit to the U.S Department of State at a U.S. embassy or consulate
- Attend your interview for J-1 status

Putting It All Together

If you're outside the U.S. and you want to come here temporarily to simply explore the landscape and check things out, you can pursue a B-1 or B-2 visitor visa, or go through ESTA and the Visa Waiver Program (VWP) and enter in Waiver-Business (WB) or Waiver-Tourist (WT) status, or get a J-1.

If you know you want to start a U.S. business, you have two primary options: B-1 business visitor visa (harder to get; stay up to 6 months at a time) or ESTA as a Waiver-Business visitor (WB) (easier to get if you qualify; stay up to 90 days at a time).

The route you decide to go will depend on what makes the most sense for you and your family. There's a lot to consider here, for example: Is your home country on the list of VWP countries? Are you likely to be subject to the J-1 212(e) two-year home residency requirement? Are you confident in your business plan yet? How soon do you need to come?

While you technically can incorporate and own a company on all of the visas we've covered in this section, do keep in mind that you can't formally work for your company on any of them, unless you're a J-2 spouse with a work permit, but even then, your stay is only temporary. There is some nuance here on which business activities do or do not count towards that restriction, so consult with an immigration lawyer when your proposed plans are defined enough to articulate.

I hope that the information in this chapter helps you land on the best next step, and my team and I are always here to answer any questions that come up along the way.

Status	Typical Visa Duration	Length of Stay	Approximate Processing Time	Can I work at my U.S. startup?
B-1 Business Visitor	10 years	6 months	3 months	No
B-2 Tourist	10 years	6 months	3 months	No
ESTA (WB/WT)	2 years	90 days	3 days	No
J-1 Trainee / Researcher	2-5 years	1-5 years based on type	3 months	No
J-2 Spouse	2-5 years	1-5 years based on type	3 months	Yes, with work permit

*See "After You Arrive"

Ready to visit? My team is here to help.

On Imposter Syndrome

You may be feeling a mental block when it comes to getting started on all of the steps involved with starting your business in the U.S.

I've been there.

Is the block there because there's just so much to do? You're swamped already trying to run your company? There's not enough time in the day, and you're overwhelmed.

What if it is actually something else?

What if you get to the U.S. to start your business... and you fail?

We might also worry: what if I actually get my dream? Will it be what I want it to be? Will I be ready to meet the challenge? Am I ready for the personal growth that will be required of me to become this future version of myself?

To go through this entire process to reach for the unknown can feel daunting. That's a fact. No success is guaranteed in life, and everything you're feeling is totally normal.

These questions come from those parts of our human brains designed to keep us alive for the survival of the species. We had to evolve to include the desire to stay safe. But our comfort zones can be limiting. They're not where the growth edges are.

We can acknowledge and thank these thought cycles for getting us to the present moment. But remember -- what got us here isn't what's going to get us there — where we want to be.

So be brave, dear reader, and when worries arise, acknowledge them with compassion and care, yet act with courage and confidence.

You can do it. Every human being deserves to reach our dreams.

We have so much potential!

CHAPTER 4

Starting With the End in Mind: I Have an Existing Business and I Want to Expand to the United States

What an exhilarating time for you and your team! Congratulations on your upcoming United States expansion and for all the growth that got you to this stage. You should be proud of what you have accomplished, and excited for what's to come.

There are lots of great reasons to expand your existing business to access the U.S market. It's U.S. is a great place to grow sales due to our economy of potential customers and investors who share a largely similar language and culture (localization isn't as necessary here). You might be interested in participating in a startup accelerator or incubator program. You might also want to access the diverse and accomplished U.S. talent pool.

In this chapter we'll cover a handful of the most promising routes for successfully bringing your startup to the U.S. if it's already started in another country.

The visas we'll cover in this chapter (L-1, O-1, E-2 and IER) are great compared to the H-1B work visa because they do not require a special minimum wage or limit how much equity you can hold.

Let's get started.

Choose Your Own Adventure

START

Have you worked on your startup in your home country for 1+ of the last 3 years?

Yes → **Skip to the L-1A Executive Visa section**

No ↓

Do you meet the requirements for an O-1A Visa?

Yes → **Skip to the O-1A Visa section**

No ↓

Do you live in a U.S. treaty country & do lots of investment & trade with the U.S.?

Yes → **Skip to the E-1 & E-2 Visa section**

No ↓

Skip to the International Entrepreneurial Parole Section

L-1A Executive Visa

L-1A visas are a great option for international founders who have already been working for their startup abroad for at least one year out of the past three years and now want to open their first office in the U.S.

Specific corporate relationships are required. For example, you can keep your parent company abroad, and open a fully-owned U.S. subsidiary. Or, you could create a branch or affiliate. It's ok if the parent company is in the U.S. and the subsidiary is abroad.

The Delaware Flip

If you already have a startup in your home country and you want to expand to the U.S. to raise venture capital, U.S. investors might be interested in you pursuing a Delaware "Flip." This corporate transactional procedure usually involves buying out the shareholders of the foreign company, compensating them with shares of the Delaware (DE) company, assigning the IP to the DE company, and making the foreign company a subsidiary of the DE company. U.S. investors tend to like this as many funds are often required to only invest in certain U.S. companies.

Other companies that have already raised significant capital in their home countries might be able to bypass the need for a "Delaware Flip" if investors are willing to directly invest in the foreign parent company. Most corporate lawyers I talk to typically recommend that founders hold off on flipping until it's required by investors and they've raised a big enough round to justify the cost.

Whether you are pre-flip, post-flip, flip-agnostic or abstaining from a flip, as long as the foreign company and the U.S. company have one of a variety of qualifying relationships, the U.S. entity will be qualified to petition for an L-1A work visa.

L-1 Qualifications

To qualify for an L-1A, you will need to show that you have secured a physical location in the U.S. and that this office will support your position within one year of your approval for the visa. Even though remote work is culturally normal today, L-1s still require a physical office.

There is some flexibility: my team has been successful in getting L-1A visas approved for companies with dedicated spaces in coworking locations. It's beneficial to have your own four walls, desks, chairs, and computers. And, your sign on the door is always a good sign!

Be prepared to submit business plans, growth models, and organizational charts as part of your application. If you receive an L-1A visa to open a new U.S. office, it will be valid for one year, at which point you will have to demonstrate you've met your growth goals. With that, the L-1A can be extended for a total of up to seven years. (For companies that are established and already have a track record of doing business in the U.S., the initial approval period for an L-1a is three years).

But what if the time comes around to renew your one-year startup L-1A and your company still hasn't found product-market fit or met its targets such as revenue? A year is a short amount of time, after all. At this point, you do have the option to apply for another one-year new office L-1A to get some extra time, or, you can always pivot to another work visa in this book.

The L-1A in recent years has been met with heavy scrutiny by administrations on both sides of the aisle. I always recommend working with an immigration attorney to help you present the strongest case possible.

L-1A Pros

- Your spouse and children under the age of 21 can join you
- Your spouse can work automatically
- No lottery
- Apply any time
- Premium Processing available for a petition decision in 15 days
- Except for North Korea, I don't think your country of citizenship matters
- Likely ok to raise venture capital in the U.S. (unlike the E-2 you don't need to maintain 50% home country ownership)
- Minimum new office investment not specified
- Dual-intent: ok to pursue green card before and after obtaining L-1
- You might also qualify for an EB-1C green card for multinational managers and executives after your company has been doing business for at least one year in the U.S.

L-1A Cons

- Evidence required to demonstrate you worked one year out of the last three at your company abroad
- You can only work for the company that petitioned you
- Increased USCIS scrutiny
- Maximum stay: 7 years

O-1A Visa

As we covered in Chapter 2, the O-1A extraordinary ability visa is another powerful work visa for founders. If you have an existing business and you want to move it to the U.S., see if you qualify for an O-1A visa before you consider other options, such as an H-1B.

Keep in mind that, like an H-1B, someone else must formally petition for you. You can set up your future U.S. company as either a parent or subsidiary of your company abroad for this one, or it can even have totally separate ownership.

In comparison to an L-1A, there is no requirement to prove anything about whether you have worked at the company abroad.

Also, an O-1A can be petitioned by an agent instead of an employer, allowing you to be self-employed or hold multiple gigs pursuant to an itinerary of services in your field.

For more information on the O-1A visa and its eligibility requirements, skip back to Chapter 2.

E-1 & E-2 Visas

E-1 visas are for "treaty traders" and E-2 visas are for "treaty investors." A treaty, in this sense, an international treaty of trade and commerce between the U.S. and your country of citizenship.

The U.S. has over a hundred immigration treaties with over eighty countries. These treaties often create reciprocity for trade and investment by nationals. For example: citizens of a country can enter the U.S. for trade or investment purposes if U.S. citizens can do the same in their country.

The earliest of these treaties was formed with the United Kingdom in 1815 after the conclusion of the war of 1812. Among various articles, it outlined rules for commerce, tax, navigation, and immigration. Uniquely, the U.K.'s treaty with the U.S. requires that E-2 applicants can prove that they are domiciled in the U.K. and will retain their home there.

The most recent immigration treaties were signed with New Zealand and Israel in 2019. Israelis were able to enter the U.S. for E-1 treaty trader purposes as of 1954, but only in 2012 was a treaty made that opened up reciprocal E-2 treaty investor status. The U.S. Department of State was able to confirm that reciprocal accommodations were made and approved E-2 treaty investor visas for Israelis starting in 2019.

The U.S. Department of State keeps an active list of treaty countries for you to reference for both E-1 and E-2 visas. Some countries only have a treaty or E-1 or E-2 status, but not both. Examples of some E-2 treaty countries include Pakistan, Germany, Israel, Taiwan, and Morocco.

Other countries, such as China and India, do not currently have the prerequisite treaties in place and their citizens are ineligible for E-1 and E-2 visas. However, let's say that a person from China has immigrated to Canada, or a person from India has immigrated to Australia, and eventually they apply for citizenship in their new home. With the Australian passport now in hand, the person born in India could apply for an E-1 or E-2, as could the Canadian citizen born in China.

E-1 visas allow individuals to enter the U.S. to carry out international trade, which can include physical goods or services like banking, insurance, tourism, and more. At least 50% of the trade must be carried out between the U.S. and your home country in order to qualify. It's also helpful to be able to demonstrate evidence of a track record of past trade completed over the last couple of years in order to qualify.

E-2 visas, on the other hand, allow founders to enter the U.S. while they invest substantial capital to build their business there. To qualify for an E-2 visa as a founder, at least 50% of your business must be owned by people or companies from your country of citizenship. This can get complicated if your startup has raised several rounds of funding from U.S. investors.

We also talked about the Delaware Flip. Keep in mind that the E-1 and E-2 visas require that the U.S. company is at least 50% owned by citizens of the treaty country. If you are doing a Delaware Flip and a future U.S. entity will own your existing startup abroad, that can be great to qualify for an E-1 or E-2, but make sure you talk to your immigration lawyer to confirm the corporate lawyer's proposal before embarking on this path. An immigration lawyer can work with your corporate lawyer to help you best structure your company for an E-1 or E-2 visa.

Although the E-2 requirements don't specify any particular minimum capital amount that must be invested to qualify for the visa, immigration officers will look for large, upfront investments in office space, equipment, and inventory for this visa, usually in the $100,000 and above range. Technically the State Department calls this the proportionality test, and you must demonstrate that a substantial amount of funds have been invested.

The investment does not have to be cash. Some founders have obtained the E-2 by transferring their IP to their U.S. company, or even by demonstrating raised funds.

Planning to hire U.S. workers for roles like sales and marketing can also be helpful to your visa approval. Already having U.S. employees or showing a business plan that includes hiring demonstrates job creation also supports your case.

Thinking of exiting your U.S. startup by selling it to a U.S. buyer? Be cautious about this if you are on an E visa. U.S. ownership might disqualify you, and you might want to complete a change of status away from your E visa to another visa such as O-1 before the sale so you can remain working in the United States.

Both E-1 and E-2 visas can range in duration from a few months to up to five years, depending on your country of citizenship. However, each admission to the U.S. in E status allows you to be physically present for up to two years at a time. Because of this, some founders enter toward the tail end of their five-year visa and then their two years of status can extend beyond this initial five-year visa period.

Applying for an E-2 visa at a U.S. embassy or consulate in your home country can be a year-long process, with each consulate maintaining different application protocols, review procedures, and interviewing timelines, so plan accordingly.

If you obtain your E-1 or E-2 through a change of status in the U.S. and then you want to depart to travel internationally, you'll have to restart the lengthy consular adjudication process from the beginning. Talk to your immigration lawyer about the best method for applying for your E visa.

E-2 Pros

- Your spouse and children under the age of 21 can join you
- Your spouse can work automatically
- No lottery
- Apply any time
- Premium Processing available for a change of status petition decision in 15 days (in U.S. only)
- Can be extended indefinitely in 2-year increments
- Employees who are citizens of the same treaty country as you are also eligible for an E-2 visa without prior work experience at your company abroad
- No foreign company required
- No foreign employment required

E-2 Cons

- You can only work for the company that petitioned you
- Be cautious about raising U.S. venture capital as diluting your company's foreign ownership below 50% can jeopardize your visa
- E-2s require a substantial investment, usually in the realm of at least $100,000
- You need to show your business is on track in order to renew

Case Study: B-1/B-2 Denial, E-2 Victory

This case study has been anonymized to protect the identity of those involved.

Borys P. grew up in Poland and always dreamed of living and working in the U.S. This eagerness, however, caused him great difficulty when he applied for a tourist visa many years ago. The consular officer believed that he did not have strong enough social and economic ties to Poland and he wasn't able to meet his burden of proof of nonimmigrant intent.

Borys eventually founded his own company in Poland and became a successful entrepreneur. He wanted to expand to the U.S., but his tourist visa experience, coupled with increased scrutiny of visa applications, left him cautious.

We advised Borys to remain in Poland while we helped him pursue an E-2 visa. Poland has an investment treaty with the U.S., and Borys was running a successful business in Poland, so this seemed like a great path forward.

We helped him structure his U.S. business to comply with E-2 requirements. Without ever stepping foot in the U.S. Borys was able to incorporate his company, rent office space, furnish the space, purchase equipment, create marketing materials, and set up payroll. At the end of the day, he had invested more than $100,000 to set up his company's U.S. office.

Next, we guided Borys through the E-2 visa requirements to make sure he presented the strongest petition possible. This included submitting business and hiring plans, growth trajectories, profit and loss statements, and more.

Before his appointment at the consulate, we helped Borys prepare for the questions he might get about himself and his business. Two days after his interview, he received his visa. The whole process only took four weeks from filing to approval!

What's next for Borys? He wants to hire American employees and create more jobs in the U.S., while also petitioning for E-2 visas so a few of his top employees can come work in the U.S. office.

International Entrepreneurial Rule Parole (IER/IEP)

If you're a founder and you can't qualify for an L-1, O-1 or E-2, then you can consider parole through the International Entrepreneurial Rule (IER). It's a pathway for entrepreneurs to come to the U.S. to demonstrate a "significant public benefit." If you get IER, you can be self-employed as a founder at your startup and your spouse can obtain a work permit.

To apply for IER, you must demonstrate that your startup will rapidly grow, create jobs, contribute to the U.S. economy, or otherwise represent "significant public benefit." You must also have received at least $264,147 from qualifying U.S. investors — a figure which is adjusted every three years, and is up for adjustment again in 2024.

There is no standard definition of "significant public benefit," but many factors are considered, such as evidence of investment, grants, revenue generation, media coverage, prior startup success, and more.

A U.S. Customs and Border Patrol (CBP) officer at an airport or other U.S. port of entry will have the final say on whether you and your family are granted IER and for how long. There is no equivalent of a "change of status" here. The CBP officer has the discretion to approve or deny your entry, so prepare in advance with your immigration attorney who can let you know the types of questions you may be asked. If you are abroad, you may have to seek a boarding foil from the State Department in your passport before travel.

CBP can permit an initial IER stay of up to 30 months. To renew parole beyond the initial 30 months, you will have to meet the IER extension requirements and file an extension application.

I believe the program has great promise and I am engaged in advocacy to improve the program's accessibility for founders. My firm and I successfully advocated to CBP to grant IER beneficiaries the full 30 months of initial stay in the U.S. Previously, CBP officers would only grant a maximum 12-month stay due to a glitch in the agency's automated system that was not fixed for a lengthy period of time. It was a huge victory for founders!

However, at the time of this writing, my founder clients have been waiting over two years to get their IER decisions; there is no Premium Processing for IER. These clients all lost interest in waiting and eventually obtained other visas such as the L-1 or O-1.

If IER is your only chance, try working with your attorney to file it concurrently with a USCIS Expedite Request based on severe financial loss with the support of or a letter from a Senator or Member of Congress. That's probably your best chance at the time of this writing for a quick adjudication.

Follow my TechCrunch column, Ask Sophie, for the latest updates — I hope to announce faster processing for IER soon!

IER Criteria

Here's what USCIS considers when evaluating IER applicants:

- Your startup should be less than 5 years old
- You should own at least 10% of your startup
- Your role should be central to the startup's operations
- Your startup should have received at least $105,659 in government awards or grants, or at least $264,147 from qualified U.S. investors within 18 months of applying
- It may help your case to show any proof of revenue generation, job creation, or any other reliable evidence that indicates your startup's potential for growth in the U.S.
- Include any relevant newspaper articles, accelerator participation, prior startup participation, patent awards, and advanced degrees as well

Putting It All Together

There are a lot of attractive and compelling options for founders who have started a successful business abroad — hooray! I mean it when I say that the hardest part is behind you. What comes next is just a matter of some organization, some paperwork, and some waiting. You've got this.

Here's a chart to help you figure out which option would best support your short- and long-term goals in the U.S.:

Status	Typical Visa Duration	Status	Extensions	Approximate Processing Time*	Is Premium Processing Available?
O-1	3 years	3 years	Unlimited in 1-year increments	1-2 months	Yes
E-1	5 years	2 years	Unlimited in 5-year visas with 2 year stays	2-3 months	Yes
E-2	5 years	2 years	Unlimited in 5-year visas with 2 year stays	2-3 months	Yes
L-1A	New office: 1 year Established office: 3 years	1 to 3 years	2-year extensions up to 7 years	1-2 months	Yes
IER	30 month authorization	30 months	Extensions up to 5 years	2+ years	No

*Without Premium Processing

Ready to expand? My team at Alcorn Immigration Law is here to help.

89

On Feelings

Are you excited about the prospect of expanding your business to the U.S.?

Take as long as you need to think about whether this is the right move for you.

But when you're ready to go for it, remember these words from Neville Goddard: the dominant of two feelings is the one expressed.

Goddard espouses that "I am healthy" is a more powerful feeling than "I will be healthy."

Because to say "I will be" is to imply "I am not now."

So when you're ready to go for it, instead of saying: "I will expand my business," say this instead:

"My business is expanding to the United States."

Now say it out loud.

Do you feel the power in that statement?

When you say "I will be," you admit to yourself that you "are not" currently at your desired state. And when we say "I am not," we reinforce this belief in our soul.

So say "I am" instead. Say it with great feeling and repeat it to yourself when the process gets difficult, or you feel stuck, because if something "is," then it just "is": it's no longer up to you.

The thing is, when you feel the reality of the "I am" state — when you really believe it — you will start living and acting accordingly, and by doing so, that desired state will arrive so much faster than you would have thought possible.

If you want to take it even further, affirm to yourself: "I have a thriving U.S. business."

To change your feelings is to change your destiny.

CHAPTER 5

Green Card Basics

Home in the U.S.

Until now, we've been talking about short-term visas that allow you to live in the United States for a limited duration and specific purpose, and how to leverage those categories to establish and grow your startup.

But now we're switching gears: it's time to make the U.S. your permanent home.

In this chapter, we'll review the green card process, define key terms, and cover the similarities between different types of green cards. Then, before moving onto startup green cards in the next chapter, we'll review the most common green card categories: family-based green cards, humanitarian green cards, and diversity green cards (in case you happen to be able to get one of those first).

After that, we'll start our in-depth exploration of the best green cards for startups and founders. In general, founders tend to gravitate towards categories that are employment-based and self-petitioned. In the next chapter, we'll cover the EB-1A based on extraordinary ability in the sciences, arts, education, business, or athletics. We'll also review the EB-2 NIW for those with an advanced degree or exceptional ability whose work is in the national interest, as well as a few other categories of note for startups. If any of these sound more up your alley, feel free to skip ahead to Chapter 6.

Key Terms

Let's take a few minutes up top to understand each part of the green card process. Here are some key terms you'll see throughout the following chapters. As always, you can turn back to Chapter 1 for a refresher on all our key terms.

- **Adjustment of Status** is the process you can use to apply for a green card when you have already been admitted to the U.S. in another status.

- **Advance Parole** is a travel document issued by USCIS that allows certain immigrants to travel outside of the U.S. and return lawfully. If you're seeking adjustment of status, you must usually apply for Advance Parole before leaving the country.

- **Concurrent Filing** refers to filing your green card petition (I-140) and your adjustment of status application (I-485) at the same time with all the required filing fees and supporting documents in one package if your priority date is current. This can speed up your green card process.

- **Current Priority Dates** are displayed on the Visa Bulletin and represent a cut-off: only those who have priority dates on or before that date can apply for an immigrant visa or adjustment of status.

- A **Medical Examination** is required for most green card applications. This exam must be completed by an authorized doctor. You can expect a review of your medical history and immunization records, a physical and mental evaluation, drug and alcohol screening, getting current on your vaccinations and tests for various illnesses and diseases. The purpose of a green card medical exam is to make sure the beneficiary has no health condition that would make them "inadmissible" to the U.S.

- The **National Visa Center** is part of the State Department and is responsible for holding green card petitions approved by USCIS until an immigrant visa number becomes available, at which point it schedules the beneficiary's immigrant visa interview and associated steps.

- **PERM** stands for Program Electronic Review Management and refers to the system used for a company to obtain a labor certification, typically the first step in an employment-based green card process.

- Your **Priority Date** is the earlier of either the date your PERM or your employment-based green card petition was filed. When you're looking at the Visa Bulletin to see if you can file, you are looking to see if your priority date is before your green card category's cut-off date.

- **Self-Petitioning** refers to the process of applying for a employment-based green card without employer sponsorship. EB-1A and EB-2 NIW green cards, which we'll cover in the next chapter, can be self-petitioned.

- The **Visa Bulletin** is a State Department (and now also USCIS) publication that shows which green cards are being processed based on priority dates, categories and countries. This resource is updated monthly to help you understand your place in the line for a green card.

There are many paths up the green card mountain, and the view from the top is the same. There are four general routes to the peak, Permanent Residence:

1. Employment, including self-sponsored, company-sponsored, and investment-based green cards

2. Family-based via marriage or other family relationships

3. Humanitarian green cards for asylees and refugees

4. Diversity lottery for people from countries with low levels of immigration

5. Next up, let's cover some helpful background relevant to all green card types.

Green Card Process

Green Card Caps

All green card categories — except for immediate relatives (the spouses, parents, and dependent children of U.S. citizens) — are limited in the number that can be issued every government fiscal year. Additionally, there is also a per-country limit of 7% of the total number of green cards available. Your country of birth has a large effect on your eligibility and wait time for a green card. Because the demand from certain countries like India or China is high, the wait times can be decades or more for individuals born there.

Priority Dates

To recap, your priority date is the date when your green card petition was filed with USCIS, and a cut-off date signifies when you can apply for your green card after your petition has been filed. Cut-off dates can be found on DOS' monthly Visa Bulletin.

Let's say you filed a green card petition on January 1st, 2015 for an F-1 Family Preference visa (more on that below) and your home country is Bulgaria. You would locate the family-sponsored preference class section in the monthly Visa Bulletin and see a table like the one below:

Family-Sponsored	All Chargeability Areas Except Those Listed	China	India	Mexico	Philippines
F1	01DEC14	01DEC14	01DEC14	01APR01	01MAR12
F2	08SEP20	08SEP20	08SEP20	01NOV18	08SEP20
F3	22NOV08	22NOV08	22NOV08	01NOV97	08JUN02
F4	22MAR07	22MAR07	15SEP05	01AUG00	22AUG02

When you're looking at the Visa Bulletin, you are looking to see if your green card category's cut-off date aligns with your priority date. If a green card category is marked with "C" it means it is "Current" and green cards are immediately available. If a category has a cut-off date beside it, only individuals with the same priority or earlier can get a green card.

As your home country is not China, India, Mexico, or the Philippines, you would focus on the second column: all chargeability areas except those listed.

You want to focus on the "F1" row, as that is the green card you petitioned for. We can see from the table that the current cut-off date for F1 visas is December 1st, 2014. This means that only those whose petition was filed on or before December 1st, 2014 are now eligible to apply for a green card.

So if your priority date is January 1st, 2015 — hang tight, your cut-off date is coming up soon!

Cross-Chargeability

Cross-chargeability refers to a process of "charging" your green card to a spouse's country of birth rather than your own. Let's say you are married and your spouse is also not a U.S. citizen : you are from Mexico, which has very high green card demand, and your spouse is from Kenya.

If their priority date is current, you can "cross-charge" your application to their priority date. To take advantage of this process, you and your spouse must file your green card applications together.

Visa Retrogression

Usually the cut-off dates on the Visa Bulletin move forward in time — but not always. The number of applicants that come in varies from month to month and this has an effect on cut-off dates. For example, if 10,000 people had a priority date of November 2014 but 100,000 had a priority date of December 2014, the Visa Bulletin may stay on December 2014 for ten times the amount of time it stayed on November 2014.

Visa retrogressions can also occur towards the end of a fiscal year as visa caps for categories or countries are approached. Sometimes a priority date that meets the cut-off date one month will not meet it the next month, so it's important to check the Visa Bulletin often. When a new fiscal year begins in October, a new supply of visas is made available and cut-off dates tend to return to their normal progression.

Adjustment of Status vs. Immigrant Visa

Most founders start working on their startup in the U.S. on another visa, like an O-1A, before they switch over to a green card. But a visa is not required for a green card. In fact, you can apply to receive a green card even if you've never set foot in the U.S. For example, if you're a founder with children you may want to go straight to a green card so your family only has to move once, and your children can pay in-state tuition at public colleges and universities —or bypass the need for F-1 status.

Each country's process is different If you are applying for a green card from outside the U.S., so you'll have to check with your local U.S. consulate for more details.

If you are already lawfully in the U.S. on another visa, you will pursue an adjustment of status and file Form I-485 (Application to Register Permanent Residence or Adjust Status), a.k.a the green card application, when your priority date is current.

Depending on if you're pursuing an adjustment of status or applying directly for an immigrant visa from outside the U.S., your process will look different. Typically you will file Form I-130, Form I-140, or Form I-526 depending on your path to Permanent Residence, followed by DS-260 (the online application for an immigrant visa). Your petition will then be with the National Visa Center until your visa interview.

If you have valid nonimmigrant status already, you can choose whether to do this process from within the U.S. or from your home country. Most people choose to do the adjustment of status process from within the U.S., which may mean you cannot leave the country until the process is complete.

How to Adjust Your Visa Status to a Green Card

Here are the steps to follow if you're in the U.S. on a visa and you want to change your status to a green card:

- Decide on the path through which you want to apply for your green card and file the associated petition:
    - Employment: Form I-140 or I-526 for EB-5 investor green card
    - Family: Form I-130
    - Asylum: Go straight to Form I-485
- Some petitions are eligible for Premium Processing and will receive a decision from USCIS within 15-45 days; for others, you may have to wait years to receive an approval. USCIS' website lists average processing times for each green card category
- Once you receive approval and your priority date from USCIS, wait until your priority date is current and then file Form I-485 (note: those petitioning for asylum do not need to wait before filing Form I-485). You have to maintain valid status up until the I-485 is filed
- If your priority date is current, you may be able to file both your petition and Form I-485 at the same time to speed up your green card process. Consult with your immigration lawyer on the best way to navigate concurrent filings. Sometimes founders prefer to get their I-140 approved with Premium Processing first before filing an I-485 but it depends on your unique situation
- Once your I-485 application is sent to USCIS, you may have to wait 6 or more months before your case is approved. Check with your immigration lawyer, but you might not be able to depart the U.S. while you are waiting.
- You will receive a receipt number from USCIS which you can use to track your green card status online on USCIS' Case Status page. Processing times vary and can be referenced online.
- During this time, you may be be required to attend a biometrics appointment, send in a medical exam, or meet with USCIS for a green card interview (more on that in Chapter 7)

Social Security Numbers

A Social Security Number (SSN) is a unique identifier issued by the Social Security Administration. It allows you to work, conduct business with a bank or financial institution, pay taxes, and qualify for certain public benefits in the U.S.

If you requested an SSN card as part of your visa application (Form DS 230 or electronic Form DS 260), then your information will be shared with the Social Security Administration so they can issue you an SSN card once you have a green card.

If you didn't request an SSN when you applied for your visa, you will have to visit a Social Security office to apply for one. Bring your permanent resident card with you as well as your birth certificate and a birth certificate for each member of your family also applying for an SSN. You should receive your SSN card within two weeks after the Social Security office receives everything they need to process your application.

But you don't have to get a green card in order to get an SSN. You can also apply for one on the same application form you use to apply for employment authorization (Form I-765). While you don't need an SSN to get a driver's license, register for school, or get private health insurance, many lawful noncitizens pursue a SSN so they can access other benefits, like federal financial aid or public health insurance.

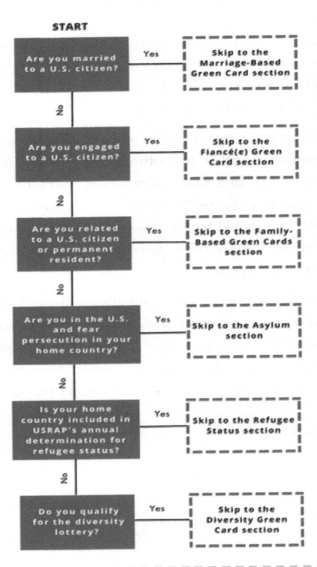

Choose Your Own Adventure

START

Are you married to a U.S. citizen? — **Yes** → Skip to the Marriage-Based Green Card section

No ↓

Are you engaged to a U.S. citizen? — **Yes** → Skip to the Fiancé(e) Green Card section

No ↓

Are you related to a U.S. citizen or permanent resident? — **Yes** → Skip to the Family-Based Green Cards section

No ↓

Are you in the U.S. and fear persecution in your home country? — **Yes** → Skip to the Asylum section

No ↓

Is your home country included in USRAP's annual determination for refugee status? — **Yes** → Skip to the Refugee Status section

No ↓

Do you qualify for the diversity lottery? — **Yes** → Skip to the Diversity Green Card section

Green Cards Through Family

The U.S. immigration system also allows for family sponsorship of green cards. Citizens and LPRs can sponsor certain family members for family-based green cards in several categories. These are subject to wait times based on category and country on the Visa Bulletin.

However, there's a fantastic exception: certain family members of U.S. citizens who are considered immediate relatives (IR) are not subject to the annual green card limits. In these situations, where the beneficiary is already physically present in the U.S., it might be possible to sponsor Form I-130 (Petition for Alien Relative) and Form I-485 (Application to Register Permanent Residence or Adjust Status) for the green card concurrently as there cannot be a backlog for immediate relatives.

Family-Based Green Cards

You can receive a green card through family in the following situations:

- You are an unmarried child under 21 of a U.S. citizen
- You are a child adopted by a U.S. citizen
- You are the parent of a U.S. citizen who is at least 21 years old

These are called "immediate relative" (IR) visas and they do not have an annual cap.

If the family members you have in the U.S. are permanent residents (not citizens), or you don't fall into one of the categories above, you may still have a path towards a family-based green card through one of the other family-based categories.

The following green cards are available through immigrant visas and adjustment of status, but may be subject to backlogs based on your country of chargeability on the Visa Bulletin:

- Unmarried son or daughter of a U.S. citizen (over 21) (≥23,400 annually)

- In order of preference: 1) spouse of an LPR, 2) child of an LPR (unmarried and under the age of 21), and, 3) unmarried son or daughter of an LPR (over 21) (≥114,200 annually)

- Married son or daughter of a U.S. citizen (≥23,400 annually)

- Sibling of a U.S. citizen who is over the age of 21 (≥65,000 annually)

Keep in mind that annual caps may change year-over-year. Once the annual cap for a given visa is met, the rest of the applicants will be processed the following federal government fiscal year, which runs from October 1st to September 30th annually.

If you are from a country with a backlogged priority date, and you qualify for other green card categories, consider those instead. You can be the beneficiary of multiple I-130 and I-140 green card petitions in parallel; you just need one to get approved and be current, through which you can get your I-485 or immigrant visa approved.

According to the September 2021 Visa Bulletin, F-4 green cards were available to those born in Mexico who had a priority date of August 1, 2000, representing an over-two-decade wait for a green card for the people currently at the front of the line. The future wait time is not necessarily predictable based on the past wait time, but this is a potent example.

How to Apply for a Family-Based Immigrant Visa through Consular Processing

Follow the steps below if you have family in the U.S. and they will consider sponsoring you for a family-based green card:

- Understand if any of your U.S. citizen family members are immediate relatives or not. If not, figure out which preference category your relationship fits into.

- Your sponsoring relative must file Form I-130 (Petition for Alien Relative) with USCIS. If you are applying from outside the U.S., wait times for the I-130 process may be around a year. If you are applying from within the U.S., expect a wait time of closer to two years. There is no Premium Processing for family-based I-130 petitions.

- Make sure your priority date is current if you are not in an immediate relative category.

- Keep your address updated if you move while you are waiting.

- Once USCIS approves the petition, they will send a notice of approval and will forward the approved petition to the National Visa Center.

- Follow the instructions from USCIS to prepare your required documents, visa fees, and appropriate medical examination records and any biometrics needed.

- Receive your visa interview appointment notification and gather any additional evidence with your attorney

- Complete your medical exam with a certified provider in a timely manner.

- Attend your immigrant visa interview.

- If all your documents are in order and the interviewing officer is satisfied with the interview, you should receive your visa within one week.

- Enter the U.S. with your immigrant visa and submit your unopened green card packet.

- Receive your I-551 card (green card) by mail.

Marriage-Based Green Cards

Many people choose to pursue a green card in various ways through marriage. For a good-faith marriage, these green cards are generally quicker, less document-intensive, and less expensive than employment-based green card routes. Whereas the fiance visa is called a K-1, recipients of a K-3 marriage visa can also bring children under the age of 21 to the U.S. under a K-4 visa and then adjust status. Alternatively, spouses already in the U.S. with a valid entry can seek adjustment of status.

There are some things to keep in mind when pursuing this green card. If you have been married to a U.S. citizen for fewer than two years when your green card is approved, you and your children will become conditional residents rather than permanent residents. Conditional residence lasts for two years, after which you must apply to remove the conditions and become a full-fledged permanent resident with a normal 10-year green card.

Affidavit of Support

The family-based green card process includes a portion called the Affidavit of Support. Your family petitioner (and any joint sponsors) will have to sign Form I-864, which essentially states that they accept responsibility for your financial wellbeing so the U.S. government does not have to. Affidavits of support are legally enforceable. This means that if you request public benefits, the agency providing those public benefits can legally request reimbursement from your spouse and any joint sponsors. The affidavit lasts until you either become a U.S. citizen or have been working for about ten years.

If your petitioner is employed, they will have to provide an employment verification letter and their most recent pay stubs and tax returns to back up the affidavit of support. If your petitioner is self-employed, they will have to provide proof of their income such as business ownership, business license, bank account, and tax returns.

Under certain circumstances, such as if your petitioner is unemployed or the household income is too low, and there are not enough savings or assets, you will need to find a joint sponsor. Your attorney can help you navigate this process. This is someone over the age of 18 who is either a U.S. citizen or green card holder. It's best to do this with somebody with whom you have already established a long-term relationship of trust.

Good Faith Relationships

During a green card process for a spouse or fiance, USCIS assesses whether a couple has a good faith marriage: is this a fraudulent sham relationship for money or to do a favor for a friend, or does the couple intend to spend their life together?

People often ask whether USCIS officers consider it a negative if an attorney goes with a couple to an interview. Actually, the contrary is true.

Knowing that the couple is represented by an immigration attorney who has already concluded that the couple married for love — and not for a green card — can make the officer's job easier, and it can provide great peace of mind to a busy founder who has a lot on their plate working on their business.

Lying to the government can have severe consequences, including and extending beyond denial for a green card petition. You may even be barred from returning to the U.S. for a decade or more if an officer determines you committed fraud, such as pursuing a marriage-based green card under false pretenses. Lying or misrepresenting your relationship is never worth it.

Fiancé(e) Green Cards

If you are the fiancé or fiancee of a U.S. citizen, they can petition you for a K-1 visa, also commonly referred to as a "fiancé visa" (as in that marvel of cinematic excellence, *90 Day Fiancé* on the TLC channel. Once you receive a K-1 visa, you have to enter the U.S. within 60 days. You will then have 90 days to get married, at which point you can apply for an adjustment of status based on marriage. Unmarried children under the age of 21 of K-1 immigrants can also be admitted under K-2 visas.

Currently, USCIS can take a year or more to process K-1 visas, and after processing is complete, you may have to wait additional time to get a visa interview at a U.S. embassy or consulate before you receive your K-1 visa. Depending on your situation, it may make more sense to get married first and then pursue a K-3 directly, but this determination fluctuates over time based on the latest processing updates. Talking to an immigration lawyer about all of your options is always the recommended next step.

Case Study: Anika S.

This case study has been anonymized to protect the identity of those involved.

My father, John Alcorn, was an immigration lawyer, and many of his stories have stayed with me to this day. This is one of those stories.

Anika S. was from an upper-class family in India and had an excellent education. Her parents found her a husband in the U.S., a man named Kamal, and it seemed like a dream come true: she was moving to California!

Preparations for the wedding were made and soon they were married. Kamal was a U.S. citizen who my dad had helped with his immigration process. Anika completed her medical exam, attended her visa interview in New Delhi, got her K-1 visa, came to the U.S., and got married. Everything had gone according to plan.

About a year and a half later, a woman came to my father's office. It turned out she was a friend of Anika's, and she was worried about her. Anika had written her a note in secret. She was being held captive as a servant by Kamal and his family, and she needed help.

My father took a deep breath and called the county sheriff's department. Unfortunately, they were not sympathetic. They asked my father if he had hard evidence of abuse. Without that, he could not prove that a crime was being committed. When he contacted the District Attorney's office, they had the same attitude.

My father could barely sleep that night. He had brought Anika to the U.S., and now she was not only miserable but also trapped. The next day, he called the sheriff's department again and told them that he was going to Kamal's house that day. He explained his plan was to knock on the door and check on Anika himself, and he was giving them a head's up in case the intervention turned violent. They sent a police officer who was waiting on the street nearby.

My Dad drove to Kamal's home and rang the doorbell several times. A police officer was waiting in a car on the street nearby with a view of the house.

After about ten minutes, Kamal's father answered the door. They didn't want to let my father in, but he insisted, and wouldn't leave. The family members raised their voices and started arguing with my Dad. Thankfully, things didn't come to blows.

Anika heard the shouts and came out of her bedroom upstairs. She saw him and he introduced himself as her immigration lawyer. He asked if she wanted to leave.

Right then and there, she packed her suitcase and left the house with my dad.

Fortunately, Anika had a cousin in New Jersey. My father drove her to LAX and helped her buy a plane ticket. She made it safely to the

East Coast and her cousin welcomed her into their home. She got a job as a computer programmer and was eventually able to rent her own apartment.

Although of course Anika and my Dad were relieved, that wasn't the end of the story. Anika had only received a 2-year conditional green card when she entered the United States. Now, it was time for the I-751 Removal of Conditions, and Kamal refused to sign the necessary papers establishing that it was a good faith marriage. Because of that, Anika was denied, and she was sent into deportation proceedings.

My father flew to New Jersey for Anika's deportation trial. He stayed up all night reviewing her files, over and over. He had memorized every fact about Anika's case, but still, something was nagging at him. Something didn't seem right.

And then, he found it, and it was hard for him to believe that he hadn't noticed this detail earlier. Even though Anika filed for a K-3 before she and Kamal had been married for two years, she had legally entered the U.S. a week after their second wedding anniversary. Therefore, the INS officer at the airport should have given her full-fledged Permanent Residence, not 2-year conditional residence.

The immigration officer made a mistake, and Anika never needed to renew her conditional residency in the first place.

My father couldn't believe Anika's good fortune. Dawn approached morning; he hadn't slept all night but he wasn't tired in the least.

This was before cell phones. So, he met Anika at the court prior to the start of the trial and was there able to tell her not to worry — everything was going to be okay. When he showed the judge the new evidence of this clerical mistake, the judge was completely taken aback, but the facts were the facts.

And the judge agreed: Anika was and had always been a permanent resident.

She was free.

Green Cards for Asylees and Refugees

While immigration law and policy is subject to the ever-changing tides of politics, it is ultimately about the human journey to freedom. The right to live as you wish, the right to be yourself and realize your potential — these rights transcend the political lines that divide countries on the map. This is why international law protects human rights and refugees, and why U.S. immigration law provides green card pathways through asylum and refugee status.

Asylum

To file for asylum, you must already be in the U.S. and be ready to demonstrate that you have experienced persecution or have a well-founded fear of persecution if forced to return to your country.

The grounds for proving asylum can be narrow, and even if you qualify, it can take years for asylum cases to get adjudicated. Eventually you can get a work permit while you are waiting, but your international travel will be limited for a long time. If you choose to pursue this route, it's key to have patience.

It's really important to work with a solid asylum immigration attorney if you choose to pursue asylum. This framework comes with many layers of legal interpretation, case law, and precedent. Also, the process changes frequently. You should pick an attorney that you will feel comfortable working with for many years.

Some founders who have experienced persecution don't want to apply for asylum from their home countries even if they qualify. A possible reason could be if they are hoping for the situation there to change and they want to return one day. Another is if their activities in the U.S. might gain notoriety and they are worried that if somehow it got leaked that they got asylum in the U.S., it could jeopardize family members back home.

However, please rest assured: attorneys are obligated to keep their client's case information confidential, and asylum officers hold applications in the strictest confidence. Even in normal non-asylum immigration situations, the U.S. government isn't allowed to disclose people's immigration details.

Some founders who timely applied for asylum as students or visitors can get frustrated waiting for this status to finally come through, and some ultimately attempt to pivot to an EB-2 NIW or EB-1A green card when they can. This strategy of pivoting and self-petitioning a green card while in asylum-pending status might in certain cases provide a glimmer of hope for a faster green card path for those stuck in long waits.

Who qualifies for Asylum?

Here are the high-level requirements for asylees to pursue asylum status in the U.S.

- You are currently in the U.S.

- You have filed for asylum within one year of entry to the U.S.

- You have not visited your home country since you filed for asylum

- You are unable or unwilling to return to your birth country due to past persecution or a well-founded fear of future persecution

- You can't live in a third country ("firm resettlement")

- Your reason for persecution is related to one or more of the following: race, religion, nationality, membership in a particular social group, or political opinion

- You are not involved in any activities that would bar you from receiving asylum, such as terrorist activity or serious crime in your birth country

Here are a few examples of situations that might qualify for asylum:

- You were fired at during a protest

- There is an active civil war or genocide against your race or ethnicity

- Your religion is excluded from political processes

- Your government has determined that you are part of a political group and you may be subject to arbitrary imprisonment

- Your reproductive health was harmed
- Certain limited situations of gang violence or conscription where the government is unable or unwilling to protect you

To apply for asylum, work with an experienced attorney. They will help you prepare Form I-589 (Application for Asylum and for Withholding of Removal). There is no USCIS fee to apply but the investment in an experienced immigration lawyer is priceless. (I do not currently accept asylum work as this is a niche specialty and my focus is founder and startup immigration cases.)

You can include your spouse and unmarried children under the age of 21 who are in the U.S. on your application. You must file within one year of your arrival to the U.S. Missing the one-year deadline may bar you from qualifying for asylum.

Once you receive asylum status, or if your asylum status application has been pending over 150 days, you can apply for a work permit. This is a standard Employment Authorization Document and it would allow you to be self-employed or form a startup. You would not need to be on payroll at your startup as proof of income is irrelevant, unlike most other immigration pathways to work as a founder.

Eventually, you will be scheduled for an asylum interview, and your attorney should attend with you. Those granted asylum are eligible to apply for a green card one year later, including your spouse and children.

If your asylum application is denied, take heart. You get a second chance in immigration court. You'll have more time to build your startup as deportation proceedings take years. Also, you have many appeal options available to you with the Board of Immigration Appeals (BIA) in addition to a petition for review with a Circuit Court of the state where you live.

Once you have asylum, if you want to travel outside of the U.S., you must apply for a Refugee Travel Document in advance with Form I-131 (Application for Travel Document). Even with this document, you should not travel back to your birth country. Doing so may put you at a high risk of having your asylum status revoked.

Here are the requirements for pursuing your green card through asylum:

- You must have been physically present in the U.S. for at least one year after being granted asylum

- You must continue to meet the definition of an asylee or continue to be a spouse or child of such asylee

- You must have not abandoned your asylee status, i.e. by leaving the U.S. while your asylum application was processing

- You must continue to be "admissible" to the U.S. The full grounds for admissibility can be found on the USCIS website. Some reasons for inadmissibility include having a communicable disease of public health significance, committing a crime in the U.S., and drug trafficking

- You must not be firmly resettled in another country other than your birth country

While you are not required to apply for a green card in order to stay in the U.S., I recommend that you do so. Depending on changes in your home country, you might no longer meet the definition of an asylee down the line and your asylum status could be revoked. Plus, after five years as a permanent resident, you can apply for citizenship. Then, you can get a U.S. passport, and you will be able to travel more freely. I usually advise against returning to the country where you were persecuted though, even as a U.S. citizen one day in the future.

Refugee Status

If you are in your home country and facing strife, and you want to be a founder in the U.S. one day, a possible option is to come here as a refugee.

Every year, the Executive Branch of the U.S. government reviews the geopolitical situation across the world and determines the U.S.'s participation in resettling existing and potential refugees. This is done via The United States Refugee Admissions Program (USRAP), an interagency program that involves multiple governmental and non-governmental partners, like the Department of Health and Human Services, the United Nations, and refugee-focused NGOs.

You have to receive a referral to USRAP to be considered for refugee status. You can receive a referral via your local U.N. High Commissioner for Refugees (UNHCR) with whom you will officially register your refugee status. You can find your local UNHCR field office here.

However, this process is very uncertain, and it might behoove you to try to find your way here through employment such as at a U.S. multinational or with an employer willing to sponsor you for an H-1B (with or without the lottery).

If you choose to go for the refugee process, the eligibility requirements for refugee status are otherwise similar to asylum status, but unlike asylum status, you can apply for refugee status even if you are not currently in the U.S. at the time of your application.

USRAP will help you fill out the necessary forms for your refugee status application and then you will have to interview abroad with a USCIS officer to determine your eligibility. Once you are in the U.S., you can apply for your spouse and unmarried children under 21 to join you with Form I-730 (Refugee/Asylum Relative Petition) within two years of your arrival to the U.S.

As a refugee, you are able to work on your startup immediately upon your arrival to the U.S., and your EAD application will be filed for you. As with asylum, be careful of travel outside of the U.S.; you will need a Refugee Travel Document.

One year after receiving refugee or asylum status, you will become eligible to apply for a green card for yourself and your qualifying family which puts you on a path towards citizenship. To pursue the green card process, you must have been present in the U.S. for at least one year since being admitted as a refugee and not had your refugee status terminated. There is no filing fee for refugees and you don't have to pay fingerprinting or biometric fees either.

Diversity Green Card Lottery

So far in this chapter, we've covered green cards for founders through non-business routes such as marriage, family, asylum, and refugees. Before we dive into employment-based green cards in the next chapter, let's spend a few pages covering the Diversity Immigrant Visa Program (DV Program), commonly known as the annual Green Card Lottery.

The DV Program makes up to 50,000 immigrant visas available every year for individuals born in countries with low rates of immigration to the U.S. This means that countries like India, China, and Mexico are not on the list.

However, people born in places like Madagascar, Bhutan and Finland usually are usually eligible. Some other countries currently eligible for a Diversity Visa in 2024 include Egypt, Afghanistan, Thailand, Albania, Germany, Australia, Costa Rica, and more. The complete list is updated annually and available on the U.S. Department of State's website.

A tip: if neither of your parents were born or legally resided in your birth country, you can also claim your parents' original countries of birth as your own in order to register for the DV program.

To apply for a diversity green card, you must register for the lottery online in the fall — usually from early October to early November — by completing Form DS-5501 (Electronic Diversity Visa Entry Form). There is no cost to register for the lottery, but be aware that you will be automatically disqualified if you register yourself more than once per year or your forms are incomplete. When people talk about a "green card lottery," they are referring to the DV Program's online lottery system.

Once you've registered online, you will get a confirmation number — don't lose it! This number is the only way to access the online system that will tell you whether or not you were selected in the lottery and are eligible to submit a green card application.

In the spring, you can start logging into the online system to get your selection details. You won't receive any notifications through email or regular mail; checking online is the only way to find out. After you enter your confirmation code, you will receive a Diversity Visa number, which you can use to determine if it's your turn to file your green card application based on the Visa Bulletin.

Here's what the DV section of the Visa Bulletin looks like:

Region	All DV Chargeability Areas Except Those Listed Separately	
Africa	50,000	Except: Algeria - 27,550 Egypt - 16,150 Morocco - 31,725
Asia	18,750	Except: Iran - 5,500 Nepal - 12,600
Europe	30,000	Except: Russia - 25,750 Uzbekistan - 8,500
North America (Bahamas)	13	
Oceania	1,150	
South America and the Caribbean	2,250	

So if your home country is Japan and your DV number is 17,302 — congratulations, you're up! All numbers up to 18,750 for people in countries in Asia (except for the countries listed in the third column, Iran and Nepal) can now file their green card applications. What are your chances of getting selected? In 2021 more than 11.8 million people applied for the green card lottery. About 125,000 names are selected every year and the first 50,000 to register after selection are granted diversity green cards. Don't fret if your Diversity Visa number is above 50,000: more than 50,000 names are drawn every year because not everyone who is selected starts or completes their green card application process. Still, this puts the odds of selection at one percent at most, so it's best to assume that you will apply for many years before being selected. In the kind-time (it sounds better than "mean"time), I recommend exploring alternate visas.

A note on family: you and your spouse can each separately apply for a Diversity Visa at the same time to increase your chances, listing each other on your registration form as well as any unmarried children under the age of 21. If either of you is selected for the lottery, you can apply for a DV green card together for your family.

How to Navigate the Diversity Visa Program

To pursue a diversity green card, you must:

- Have been born in a country on the list of countries designated by the State Department as having a low rate of immigration to the U.S.

- Have at least a high school education or two years of work experience within the past 5 years in an occupation that requires at least two years of experience or training

- Enter the diversity lottery online in the fall (October - November) and keep track of your confirmation number

- In May, use your confirmation number to check if your application has been randomly selected. If you have been selected, you may be able to apply for a Green Card

- If you have been selected, you must then complete your immigrant visa and alien registration application (Forms DS-260) or I-485 Adjustment of Status and other associated forms and print out your confirmation page

- Make sure to submit any necessary supporting documents (such as birth certificates, military records, marriage certificates, etc.), complete your required medical examination, and prepare for your scheduled embassy or consular interview

- Attend your green card interview

- After your interview, you will be notified if your visa application has been approved or denied

Putting It All Together

At the top of this chapter we talked about the main paths to permanent residence. It's complex though, isn't it? Within each of those three categories, there are a variety of sub-options.

We covered the green card process from a bird's eye view and then zoomed in on family-based green cards and asylum and refugee status, as well as diversity green cards and the green card lottery.

Check out this table to help you decide if any of these green card options make sense for you. See you in the next chapter!

Green Card Path	Requirements	Approximate Processing Time
Immediate Relative	Have an immediate relative that is a U.S. citizen	1-2 years
K-1 Fiance	Get engaged to a U.S. citizen	2-3 years
K-3 Spouse	Get married to a U.S. citizen	2-3 years
Family-Based Preferences 1-4	Have a non-immediate relative that is a U.S. citizen or an immediate relative that is a permanent resident	2-3 years (or decades!!) depending on the category and country
Asylum	Be in the U.S. with a history or well-founded fear of persecution in your birth country	1-2 years after having asylum 1 year
Refugee	Live in a country that USRAP determines eligible for refugee status application	1-2 years after being a refugee 1 year
Diversity Visa Lottery	Be born in a country with a low rate of immigration to the U.S.	1-2 years, after winning the lottery

On Patience

You started your business abroad, or you've put together a rock-solid business plan and want to launch it in the U.S. You want the freedom to create and to reap the economic rewards, and you want it now!

Not everyone can do what you've done. To get this far, you've had to be more disciplined, more thoughtful, and more hardworking than many others.

You've had to have a bias towards action.

And now, as you go through the immigration process to come to the U.S., the periods of waiting can far outweigh the periods of action.

So, how do we sit with this waiting?

First, be strategic, and read the chapters on other nonimmigrant visas to figure out if you can qualify for a visa first before you start the green card process.

However, once you're awaiting your green card, internalize that this process can take years. And in the kindtime (the gentle meantime), you can explore other paths, or focus on your business, but at the end of the day, you still have to do a whole lot of waiting.

It can feel like a curse sometimes. The in-between state, neither here nor there, can feel interminably long.

We are impatient.

We want to get going! Do something! Take action!

We dislike waiting, but even more, we dislike uncertainty.

But here's the secret: there's nothing you can do about it.

Does that feel like relief? Because it should.

Much of this journey is out of your hands, and that's okay.

Tell yourself: I can't control everything.

Tell yourself: this process isn't mine to control.

There's a beauty in this too, no?

And iIf you don't feel that way yet, consider this a prime opportunity to finally take up that daily meditation practice you've been stalling on!

CHAPTER 6

Startup Founder Green Cards

EB-1A, EB-2 NIW, and More

Finally, we've arrived at the main pathway to permanent residence we're going to cover in this book: employment-sponsored green cards.

Now that you know the basic lay of the land, I can tell you: the best option for most startup founders and other professionally accomplished individuals wanting immigration freedom in the U.S. tends to be either an EB-1A green card for extraordinary ability or an EB-2 NIW green card for work in the national interest. For certain other founders, the EB-1C for multinational managers and executives can also be helpful. All of these categories are based on your professional accomplishments and expertise.

The main reasons my founder clients love these categories are:

1. You can self-petition; there is no need to get married or wait for an employer to sponsor you.

2. There is no PERM process; you can own as much equity in your startup as you want, and you save a year or more of your time.

3. The EB-1 is the fastest preference category, potentially saving people from India and China decades of waiting.

In general, there is a backlog for green cards because more people apply each year than the number available, as seen in the Visa Bulletin. Many people from India and China are waiting decades for their company-sponsored EB-2 and EB-3 Priority Dates to become current. According to pre-pandemic research from the Cato Institute, those from India may face an EB-2 wait time of over 150 years!

However, the Employment-Based, First Preference (EB-1) category is the most important work-based green card category and therefore has the shortest wait times that reset every October.

When should you file? If your Priority Date is current, you can either choose to file your I-485 first with Premium Processing and wait for an approval and then file your I-485, or you can concurrently file. Some of our clients whose Priority Dates are current choose to apply for both an EB-1A and EB-2 NIW at the same time. Much of the evidence, including the letters of recommendation can be similar and can be prepared properly for both.

Let's explore your options.

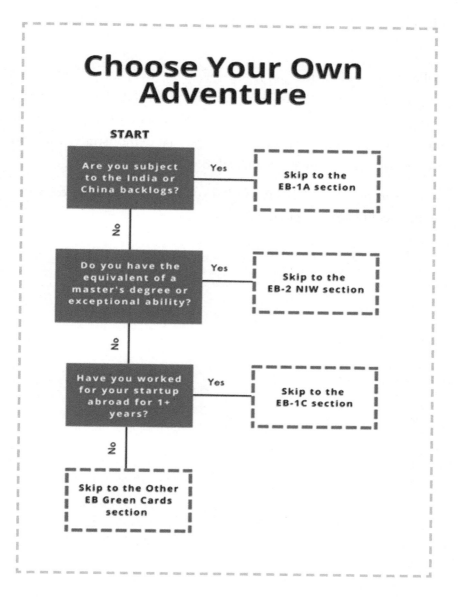

EB-1A Green Cards

The EB-1A is often the fastest way to get a green card. This matters especially if you and your spouse were both born in India or China.

This category can overwhelm people, so before we dive in, please know this: you definitely don't have to win the Nobel Prize or an

Olympic Gold to get an EB-1A green card. The vast majority of recipients haven't.

Folks who are at the very top of their field in science, arts, education, business, or athletics are eligible for EB-1A green cards. To qualify, you must receive a major, nationally or internationally recognized award, or meet other criteria that demonstrates that you are recognized and highly regarded in your field.

You can apply for an EB-1A by filling out Form I-140 with evidence of the qualifications below.

Qualifications for an EB-1A Green Card

To qualify for an EB-1A, you must meet at least three of the following ten criteria:

- You have received a nationally or internationally recognized prize or awards for excellence. These awards should be post-university level and could even include things like VC funding, pitch competitions, and international hackathons

- You are a member of associations in your field that are difficult to get into, such as invitation-only business clubs, participation in accelerators or incubators, and even advisory roles for other startups.

- Articles have been printed about you in professional or major trade publications, other major media, or books. This can include citations to your work. (However, press releases that were never published in a major publication and student-run university publications, and often company newsletters usually don't count).

- You have judged the work of others, either individually or on a panel, beyond a university-level competition. Serving as a judge for a hackathon, being a venture scout, or judging a startup pitch competition might suffice.

- You have made major contributions to your field as proven through national or international media coverage, a significant number of citations on peer-reviewed articles, or the usage of your work by others through contracts, licensed technology, and patents.

- You have written articles that have appeared in professional, scientific, or major trade publications or other major media, such as through Forbes Council.

- Your work has been displayed at artistic exhibitions or showcases. In the tech world, this can even apply to many UI/UX designers.

- You have a critical or leading role in your company, i.e. founder or CEO, although non-C-level employees can also qualify depending on their responsibilities.

- You command a high salary compared to others in the field (often top 10% for your role, level and geography). Equity valuation can be considered here.

- You have achieved commercial success in the performing arts (this may not apply to you as a startup founder).

USCIS typically processes EB-1A petitions in less than a year, but Premium Processing is available for a 15-business-day decision.

But while I-140s can be adjudicated rather quickly for EB-1As with Premium Processing, the determining factor for how long it takes to get this green card is often the I-485 (Adjustment of Status Application) processing time. Depending on your jurisdiction, once your Priority Date is current it can take up to two years to get an interview scheduled, and there are similar (or longer) processing times for immigrant visas at consulates.

EB-1A Case Study: Xiaoyin Qu

In just a few years, Xiaoyin Qu went from working as a product manager at Facebook and Instagram to leading her own multi-million dollar startup and winning spots on the Forbes 30 Under 30 in 2021 and *Inc.*'s third annual Female Founders 100 list in 2020.

Born and raised in China, Xiaoyin moved to California to attend Pomona College. After graduating with her bachelor's in economics and computer science, she began working for Facebook, first on OPT and then on a STEM OPT extension.

Facebook entered her in the annual H-1B lottery and she was selected the first time — a feat of luck. Shortly after she received her H-1B, Facebook was able to sponsor her for an EB-3 green card. "That was a really long process," Xiaoyin said. "I did the calculations and I would be waiting for at least another six years [for the EB-3]. It was a crazy number." Since then, wait times have only expanded for people born in Mainland China and India.

Xiaoyin worked at Facebook for three more years before deciding to go another, quicker route: the EB-1A. Her project management skills kicked in as she focused on bolstering her portfolio of accomplishments to meet the rigorous requirements.

"I wrote a lot about product management and my experiences and submitted articles everywhere," she says. A media company in China became interested in what she had to say and invited her to be a regular columnist. Eventually, her popular product management columns led to her book, "Building World-Class Products, 36 Tips from Silicon Valley," which became a bestseller in China. Online courses based on her book followed.

"I really wanted the freedom to start my own company. That was a big motivation," said Xiaoyin. "Without the proper immigration status, you can't do anything."

The EB-1A cleared the path for Xiaoyin to launch Run the World, an online events and networking platform that has secured around $15 million from investors like Andreesen Horowitz as well as celebrities Will Smith and Kevin Hart.

Based on her experience, Xiaoyin offers this advice to entrepreneurs: "A lot of times you don't have a role model—and that's okay. Be the role model yourself. Do something that no one thought was possible!"

I was lucky enough to be interviewed by Xiaoyin in 2023 about what founders and their families can do to mitigate the impact of layoffs on their ability to stay in the U.S.; listen in here.

EB-2 NIW Green Cards

The qualifications for an EB-2 NIW (National Interest Waiver) are less stringent than for an EB-1A. For an EB-2 NIW, you only have to show that you have an advanced degree or exceptional ability and your work or skills will benefit the U.S.' national interest.

To pass the advanced degree or exceptional ability requirement, you must meet one of the following three criteria:

- Have an advanced degree (such as an MBA, MS or Ph.D.)
- OR have a bachelor's degree and at least five years of experience in your field
- OR have at least 3 of the following:
  - Another degree or certificate in your field
  - 10 years full-time experience in your field
  - A specialized license or certification
  - A high salary or remuneration
  - Membership in professional organizations
  - Recognition in your field
  - Other comparable evidence

Next, to show your future work will be in the national interest, you must demonstrate that your work:

- Has substantial merit or national importance
- You are well positioned to advance the proposed endeavor
- On balance, it would be beneficial to the United States to waive the requirements of a job offer, and thus the labor certification because it will likely creating jobs or substantially contributing to the economy

It's not a stretch to argue that founding your company will help create jobs in the U.S. and you can include a business plan as well. Keep in mind that you don't need to prove your case beyond a reasonable doubt — you just need to provide a "preponderance of evidence" that it's more likely than not that your work is extraordinary, exceptional, or in the national interest.

Like an EB-1A, you can self-petition for an EB-2 NIW and it does not require a lengthy PERM process. As of 2023, Premium Processing is also now available for EB-2 NIWs. But if you are from a country with high levels of immigration to the U.S., like China or India, you will likely face longer wait times compared to the EB-1A because of backlogs in the Visa Bulletin.

In some cases, you can speed things up by using a Priority Date from a previous employment-based I-140 in the EB-1, EB-2 or EB-3 categories or look at cross-chargeability based on your spouse's country of birth. When your Priority Date is current you can also shave some time off the back end by submitting both your I-485 (adjustment of status application) and I-140 (green card petition) concurrently.

Great news about the EB-2 NIW — in 2023, President Biden updated the USCIS guidance, making it even easier for founders to qualify.

EB-2 NIW Case Study: Pantelis Kalogiros

Entrepreneur and software engineer Pantelis Kalogiros gets to live his dream — but his dream didn't come easy. As a young child in Greece, he longed to move to Silicon Valley to found his startup. In 2010, as Greece's government debt crisis continued to drag on and with military service looming, he decided to drop out of college and leave the country altogether.

"I was disillusioned with the situation in Greece," explained Pantelis, who had been unable to return to his home country for eight years after leaving. "The economic crisis made things quite bleak. I was lucky enough to have a very good job in Greece, but I wanted to escape."

He worked on a prestigious computer vision research project in Silicon Valley with three other computer science, artificial intelligence, and robotics experts. In 2014, they founded Fyusion to solve complex problems with 3D computer vision technologies and AI. Their spatial photography app and patented new file format called ".fyuse" enabled users to capture and share interactive 3D images using a smartphone or standard digital camera.

But to remain in the U.S. and continue growing the company he co-founded, Pantelis needed permanent residence.

"I thought that without a bachelor's degree, it would be extremely difficult to get a green card, and I could not go back to Greece because I had the military issue hanging over my head," Pantelis said. "People looked at my case and told me it's impossible. I felt depressed and defeated."

I remember the first time I chatted with Pantelis in my office. My confidence that he could get an EB-2 NIW without a Bachelor's Degree blew him away!

My legal argument: as a rapidly growing startup, Fyusion was creating important technology as well as generating significant revenue and creating jobs that benefited the U.S. economy. Ultimately, Pantelis not only got his green card, but in 2021 he also got to celebrate Fyusion's acquisition.

Pantelis said that cultivating a mindset of risk-taking and stepping out of his comfort zone was instrumental in achieving his dreams.

"I don't want to regret not doing something, so I do it even if it terrifies me. If I fail, that's okay. I will try again and use the experience to build something in the future," he said. "There are no opportunities without risk."

EB-1C Green Cards

While EB-1As and EB-2 NIWs are my personal favorites for founders, I see many founders take advantage of the EB-1C pathway if we can show they transferred from working at an international office of their company to employment in the U.S. for a year.

Although a CEO and startup founder can qualify, the I-140 cannot be self-petitioned. Therefore, keep in mind that the viability of your I-140 depends on the existence of your startup and your role continuing.

Qualifications for the EB-1C Green Card

To qualify for an EB-1C, you must:

- Demonstrate you served as a manager or executive of a related company (parent, subsidiary, branch, affiliate) abroad for at least 1 year out of the 3 years prior to your arrival to work for a qualifying employer

- Currently work for a related U.S. company that has been doing business for at least 1 year at least 1 year old

- And you have a managerial or executive role

EB-1Cs can be a great option as they only have small backlogs from time to time, just like EB-1A. The EB-1C shares many of the same requirements as the L-1 for intracompany transferees coming to work in managerial, executive or specialized knowledge roles (covered in Chapter 4), so some founders chose to change their status from an L-1A to an EB-1C once they arrive in the U.S.

However, there is no requirement to have an L-1 prior to getting an EB-1C, so the EB-1C could even follow another visa type like an O-1A.

Other Employment-Based Green Cards for Founders

While the EB-1A and EB-2 NIW are my favorite company-sponsored green cards for founders because they allow you to self-petition, it's worth noting a few other options before we continue.

There are several company-sponsored green card categories. Your attorney is best positioned to help determine which is the right fit for you. While not as common for founders as EB-1A or EB-2 NIW, I've highlighted a few in the table below.

The EB-1B is fast — like the EB-1A and EB-1C, mainly because it doesn't require waiting a year or more for the PERM process. Although it requires a job offer in a research role at a startup with other researchers, it's not an obstacle if the beneficiary holds significant founder-level equity in the startup.

The EB-2 and the EB-3 are the standard company-sponsored green card processes and include the PERM process. In addition to the longer wait time with PERM, another significant factor is that founder-level equity, or even founding engineer-level equity, might not withstand the Labor Department's scrutiny in the PERM process. Hence, even if a startup is willing to petition one of these for an employee like a CTO, they might not qualify based on their equity plan.

Category	Description	Self-Petition?	Sponsorship	PERM?	Premium Processing	Significant Equity
EB-1B	Professors and researchers	No	Employer	No	45 Days	Permissible
EB-2	Individuals with advanced degrees	No	Employer	Yes	15 Days	Obstacle
EB-3	Skilled, professional, or other workers	No	Employer	Yes	15 Days	Obstacle

Putting It All Together

We've covered seven company-sponsored green cards in this chapter. You know which two I prefer, but what about you? I hope the chart below helps you consolidate the main pathways we covered this chapter and take your next step with confidence.

EB-1A, EB-1C, & EB-2 NIW

	EB-1A	EB-1C	EB-2 NIW
Basis	Extraordinary Ability	Multinational Manager & Executive	National Interest
Self-Petition	Ok to self-petition	Not possible	Ok to self-petition
PERM	Skip PERM	Skip PERM	Skip PERM
I-140 Premium Processing	15 Days	45 Days	45 Days
Rigor	More rigorous	Less rigorous	Less rigorous
How helpful is it if you're from India or China?	Extremely advantageous; you can save decades	Extremely advantageous; you can save decades	Helpful to get a first priority date or with a current Priority Date or Cross-Chargeability

How Do I Become Qualified?

If you know you're at the beginning of your journey and you definitely want to build your accomplishments for an EB-1A, EB-2 NIW, or both, Alcorn Law offers an online class called Alcorn Academy of 15 video modules that go in depth on each of the visas' requirements.

Not sure if you're ready for an EB-1A or EB-2 NIW yet? We also offer a service at Alcorn Law called Legal Launch. We'll help you determine if you qualify for an EB-1A, and if not, we'll give you personalized and tailored recommendations so you can work towards qualifying.

Get that green gold! Start your permanent residence.

On Celebration

Have you heard of tall poppy syndrome?

It originates from the story of a Roman king who, to advise his son on how to rule, took a stick and swept it across his garden, cutting off the heads of the tallest poppies that grew there.

Tall poppy syndrome is a cultural belief that sticking out in any way — by achieving success, by being your extraordinary self — is "asking" the universe to cut you down.

It's an old belief that tells us that if we display hubris, that if we don't humble ourselves appropriately, we'll lose everything that we've built.

Many cultures are based on this — and it's one of the reasons why Silicon Valley stands out in the world as a beacon of light and hope for founders, where they can be celebrated and not reprimanded for their drive and ambition.

In other cultures, it's as if celebrating our accomplishments jinxes us. If we acknowledge our success, or enjoy it too much, we may worry that everything might disappear in an instant.

Many people I work with who qualify for an EB-1A or an O-1A for extraordinary ability are very humble people and extremely modest.

They also tend to underestimate their abilities and achievements, both because they have higher aspirations for themselves and because they come from cultures in which you need to vastly over-deliver in order to admit that you accomplished anything.

But the U.S. is different.

Here, we celebrate influencers, thought leaders, and people who pulled themselves up into wealth "by their bootstraps." That's the American dream.

And because of our culture that celebrates risk taking and even rewards those who admit failure — second-time founders receive a lot of investment, folks! — Silicon Valley exists.

I know it can be uncomfortable to put everything you've done down on paper, ask for those recommendations, and boast about what you've accomplished. You might feel guilty, ashamed, or even fearful to recognize your success.

This could feel like denial, procrastination, or other forms of resistance.

So let's try something new.

Imagine the fast-forwarded future version of yourself: totally successful, life goals achieved. Feel your chest puffed out and your chin high. Imagine your hands on your hips.

You feel successful, powerful, and worthy.

Now imagine this persona through the immigration process, not "you."

And yet, of course, it is you.

CHAPTER 7

Interview Prep

Congratulations! At this stage, you already decided on your immigration strategy and you even prepared and submitted your forms and evidence. You're so close, and the hardest part is officially behind you. Now, you just have to get through the final step: your interview.

While an interview may seem intimidating, all you have to do is show up prepared and be yourself. This chapter is going to help you do just that.

Recap Your Progress

You've done a lot of work to get to this point. Let's review the steps to get here!

1. **Decide your goal.** Are you coming to the U.S. on an immigrant or nonimmigrant visa? Do you want to explore school, starting a business, working for somebody else? What's your budget? The prior chapters will help you assess which immigration status makes the most sense for your short- and long-term goals and whether to pursue your outcome abroad or within the United States.

2. **Talk to a lawyer.** What makes a good lawyer? I put together 67 questions to ask your immigration lawyer to help you navigate this process. Refer back to Chapter 1 for a refresher.

3. **Prepare your documents.** Work with your immigration lawyer to prepare the necessary documents, questionnaires, forms, evidence, medical exams, photographs, filing fees, and more that you need to apply for your visa or green card. Your lawyer will give you a detailed and up-to-date checklist, answer your questions, review your information, and write compelling legal arguments for why you qualify.

4. **File with the government.** Your lawyer will file and track all your documents, receiving duplicate copies, and notify you about government actions, decisions, expiration dates, and next steps.

5. **Keep in touch with your lawyer about life changes.** Has any of your info changed since you filed? Talk to your lawyer if you are considering moving, are getting married or divorced, having a child, changing jobs or any other life changes. Your lawyer will advise you and help make adjustments.

Depending on what you applied for, the time you wait to hear back will vary. If there's no interview required, you'll likely either receive an approval, rejection, or request for evidence (RFE) next, which your lawyer will help you navigate.

If there is an interview, your preparations will vary depending on if you filed for an immigrant or nonimmigrant visa, you're interviewing for an adjustment of status in the U.S., or you're seeking a nonimmigrant or immigrant visa at a U.S. Consulate abroad.

Ace Your Interview

Here we go: you have an interview coming up for your visa or green card, and you want to ace it.

What will be asked?

How should you prepare?

Let's start with the obvious: an interview with any immigration official is a high-stakes undertaking with implications for your future visa or green card status. Immigration officials have the discretion to decide whether or not to grant you a nonimmigrant or immigrant visa and their notes about you are available for all other officers to see. They can bar you from the U.S. or send you to immigration court. If you are interviewing at a Consulate or U.S. Embassy, the State Department Officer has broad discretion and there is little oversight about their decision.

But here's the thing: immigration officers are people, just like you and me. They have families, hopes and dreams. They have good days and bad days. They have personalities and worldviews shaped by their own unique experiences.

The State Department and Homeland Security officers I interacted with try to do their jobs to the best of their ability. They take an oath to ensure that they will uphold our country's values and protect the United States. Their duty is to ensure that you're eligible for whatever you're applying for, you're not trying to game the system or overstay your visa, and you're safe to be allowed into the country.

The basic goals of any immigration interview are typically to: determine your eligibility, verify your info, clarify any discrepancies, request additional background, and ensure your admissibility (eg. criminal history or immigrant intent with a nonimmigrant status).

You should always answer any questions with honesty and integrity. Try to stay calm, cool and collected. Try to be clear and concise (don't appear secretive, but don't ramble). It's ok to briefly describe your plans for what activities you intend to pursue on your upcoming visa or green card.

Talk to your lawyer in advance about how to discuss prior denials, overstays, or any other challenging immigration history to determine how to best explain whatever happened.

A State Department interview at a Consulate or Embassy might be as short as 1-2 minutes. An adjustment of status interview with USCIS in the States usually lasts about 15-20 minutes.

Sample Embassy or Consulate Questions

Depending on your reasons for coming to the U.S. and the visa or green card category you pursue, you might be asked some of the questions below during your State Department interview:

- What is the purpose of your visit to the U.S.?
- Have you been to the U.S. before?
- What do you do?
- Where do you work?
- Will you be working while you're in the U.S.?
- Who is paying for your visit?
- Where are you visiting?
- How long do you plan to stay?
- Do you have any relatives in the U.S.?
- Is there a chance you will extend your stay?
- Will you be returning to the U.S. after this trip?
- Will you be traveling with anyone?
- Can you provide evidence you'll leave the U.S. at the end of your trip?

If you can bring your lawyer with you to the USCIS interview, I recommend doing so as well. While you can't bring a lawyer with you to a consular interview abroad, you can bring one with you for an interview with USCIS within the U.S. and they can also appear via telephone if the office has COVID-19 restrictions. Having an experienced lawyer at your side — or with your family if they are being interviewed separately — can give you peace of mind. If you need an interpreter, USCIS also allows them to join interviews, usually via telephone.

While the interviewer might tell you that you've been approved at the end of your interview, that doesn't always happen. Depending on your visa or green card type, you might have to wait up to 1-4 months to receive the results of your interview. So hang tight!

Here are some additional tips:

Before Your Interview

Review your submitted applications and supporting documents. Be sure you remember what you did, where you were, and when things happened in your life. Some people don't naturally recall these types of details and need to practice them.

If you notice any inaccuracies or if anything has changed since the time of submission, talk to your immigration attorney about making changes. If you're unsure about any of the contents of your documents they can help with that, too.

Having all the proper documentation available will not only make your interview smooth but it will also help you feel more at ease. Depending on your interview type, you might be required to bring:

- Interview appointment notice
- Your passport and any expired passports
- Government-issued photo ID such as a driver's license
- Social Security Card
- Birth Certificate
- Originals of any supporting documents you submitted, like a marriage or birth certificate
- Proof of income
- A photograph of you from the last six months
- Your travel itinerary, if relevant

- An employment letter from your employer and recent pay stubs from the last three months
- Recent financial documents such as pay stubs and taxes
- If you're a student, bring your latest school transcripts, I-20, and other proof of enrollment

If any of these documents are in a language other than English, you might need to get them translated. Keep your documents well-organized.

Of course, your specific documents will vary. For example, if you are entering the U.S. to seek medical care, you would also want to bring a letter from a physician in the U.S. expressing a willingness to treat you, or a medical diagnosis detailing the nature of your ailment. If you are coming to take part in a startup accelerator program, you'll want to include your official acceptance and invitation from that program. Talk to your attorney if you have any questions about what to bring or when to show it.

Your attorney will practice the interview questions with you so you feel prepared and confident.

Take note of the current COVID precautions described in your interview appointment notice. Look up the location of your interview and consider making a trip there ahead of time to scout out your transportation and parking.

Getting to Your Interview

Dress professionally. Allow ample time for transportation and parking. Plan to arrive at least thirty minutes early, because you will need time to go through security. Be aware that you can be under audio and video surveillance in any government building.

Bring your valid government identification and interview appointment letter with you. You will show these to the front desk before you go through security. After security, locate the check-in desk and present these documents. You'll be instructed on where to wait for your officer to call you for your interview.

Don't forget to leave your phone in the car, turn it off, or silence it.

It's common to wait a little while to be called for your interview, but if you find yourself waiting over an hour, I recommend you return to the check-in desk and request an update.

When your officer is ready to see you, usually your ticket number will be called.

During Your Interview

At a USCIS interview, your officer will put you under oath. You will be asked to confirm that everything you say during the interview is the truth. It is a crime to lie under oath.

If you are interviewing with USCIS, you can have an attorney with you or dial them on the phone.

When answering questions, be courteous and use formal language like "officer" and "ma'am" or "sir." Avoid slang like "yeah" or "nah" in favor of the more formal "yes" or "no."

Let the officer complete each question before answering. Pause, take a deep breath, and make sure you understand the question. If you need clarification, please ask.

When you answer, I typically recommend providing the minimum amount of information necessary to honestly and fully answer the question, and to avoid engaging in unnecessary conversation.

As my dad always used to say: "If it's a yes or no question, give a yes or no answer!"

Avoid tangents, and don't provide information that wasn't specifically requested unless advised so by your attorney.

You don't need to provide documents unless specifically requested by the officer. If the officer requests a document, only provide that document.

After Your Interview

At the end of your interview, your officer will tell you that it's complete. They might approve your application on the spot or request more information or time to make a decision.

Always request to have something in writing at the end of the interview which reflects the results of the interview. With USCIS, often the officer can take up to four months to make an official decision.

If your application is approved, you will usually receive your approval notice in the mail, along with any relevant materials. If the officer needs more information, you'll typically receive a Request for Evidence notice in the mail with next steps.

If you are called in for a second interview, you absolutely want a lawyer to help you not just prepare but over-prepare.

Once a couple came to me for legal help because they had gone through their first interview without a lawyer and were now suspected of marriage fraud. The couple didn't have a lot of shared receipts or photographs, and never had children. Their second interview was looming and they needed help.

I asked them questions about their life and explained how we needed to establish that they had a good faith marriage. Their demeanor changed when I asked them if they had kids, or planned to. That's when it came out: they were actually going through IVF, and had already invested over $100,000 in the process.

They had no idea that this detail was relevant to their visa process. However, this was highly compelling evidence that they had a good faith marriage, and I was able to help them get a quick approval.

Having a lawyer from the get-go is helpful to both understand what's actually going on and tease out which information about your life is legally significant.

Case Study: Mandy Feuerbacher

Mandy Feuerbacher is a former U.S. State Department Consular Officer and immigration attorney with a focus on helping immigrants prepare for their consular visa interviews. She served as a consular officer for seven years in Beijing, China; Matamoros, Mexico; and Hong Kong. During that time, she interviewed over 100,000 people for visas.

After her time with the State Department, she couldn't shake the feeling that her experience as a consular officer could be put to better use to help people navigate the often-murky consular process.

Mandy's Advice for Consular Interviews

"Consular officers are actually very supportive of people going to the U.S. for legitimate reasons. And pretty much every consular officer I knew took their job very seriously... I think it's just difficult because the officer is there to subject this applicant to the law. And the law is to make sure your average nonimmigrant visa applicant doesn't have immigrant intent."

But while the job is simple, and people come in with good intentions, it can be easy for consular officers to get jaded after a while.

"It's kind of a stressful journey. You go into this role really believing everybody and trusting everybody... but then you start doing things like 'Okay, this person says they're only taking a week-long trip, I'm going to check back in a couple months'... and when you realize that 90% of the people did not go back, that can be a little stressful, and it makes you kind of emerge disheartened, and question your own gullibility and whether or not you are actually doing a good job. So you do go through this process and become a little more cynical over time."

How does the State Department handle this cynicism? What standards are in place? According to Mandy, "we go through a very intensive process called visa norming. The State Department really wants each consular officer to be making the same decisions, which is very difficult... I know some of my colleagues approved everybody and trusted everybody, and we also had consular officers who were a lot more skeptical... You never know what kind of consular officer you're going to get."

But while you can't control your consular officer, you can control how much you prepare for your consular interview in advance.

"Be very proactive during the visa interview process. And I don't mean just paying attention to the question and answering the question directly. That's important, too. But I mean offering up information that is really important for the consular officer to know in order to make their decision. At my law firm, when my team of former visa officers works with clients, once we fully understand a client's situation, we tell them to weave in that information that the consular officer may never even ask them about, but we know it's very important for them to know."

The consular interview is high stakes. "It's really not worth the risk to hope that it all turns out okay, or rely on a consular officer's good mood that day," Mandy said. "You are told, especially for nonimmigrant visas, that you can apply again. But the reality is that every time you interview for a visa, that's put in a record, and notes are going to be taken about your interview... and that record will be there for consular officers to see for all subsequent interviews, even if it's for a different visa category. So it's a very important interview."

The key is to prepare, prepare, prepare. You can listen to my full interview with Mandy here.

Putting it All Together

Don't sweat about your upcoming interview. As long as you have your documents in order and you've prepared, it should go great. Run through the sample questions above a couple times with your immigration lawyer, and make sure you have a plan to address any potential concerns before they come up. Your interview will go by quickly, and my fingers are crossed that you get the answer you're hoping for!

When you are approved, make sure to take the time to talk to your attorney and fully understand your approval. Is there an expiration date? When do you need to renew, if at all? What obligations or duties do you have to fulfill in order to qualify for that renewal? This will give you clarity for your next chapter.

On the Power of Why

"When a 'why' is clear, those who share that belief will be drawn to it and maybe want to take part in bringing it to life. If that belief is amplified, it can have the power to rally even more believers to raise their hands and declare, 'I want to help.'"

This quote is from Simon Sinek's book "Start With Why," which talks about how to inspire others with your dream.

So, what is your dream?

Should an immigration official care about it?

Maybe, or maybe not.

If your dream is to increase product efficiency, for example, they probably won't care.

But my guess is: that's not your dream.

Because your dream isn't "what" you're doing, it's "why" you're doing it.

There's a monumental difference here.

What's your "why"?

Do you want to bring people peace of mind? Do you want your fellow citizens of the world to be healthier and more able to thrive?

Your "why" is magnetic, and urgent.

It speaks not only to the minds of others, but also to their hearts.

An immigration officer's job is subjective. This can be a good thing.

Be your authentic self and embody your undeniable "why."

This is the most compelling, effective way you can show up for yourself.

CHAPTER 8

Uncertainty and Its Navigation

The unexpected is part of life. We can do everything within our power to keep a ship on course, but we can't control the moon and its tides or the wind and its waves. Some things are not in our control, for example, a global pandemic, the President tweeting to halt immigration, or a weird economy.

Many of the challenges we encounter can be met through patience and the passage of time. Others take a more active approach. Remember: you have options.

In this chapter, I'll talk about some common immigration situations that can lead to uncertainty and how you can navigate them with confidence.

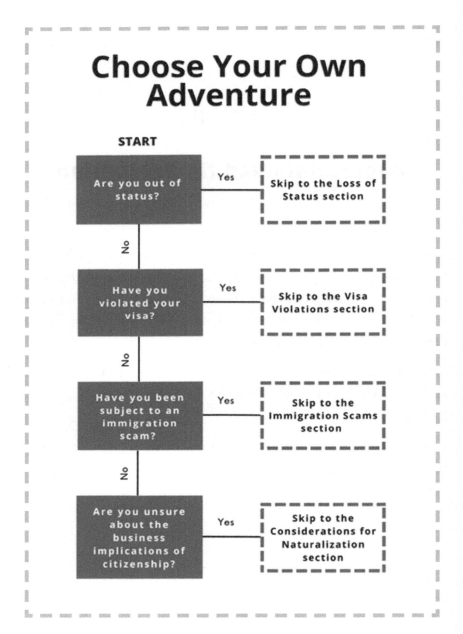

Key Terms

When we talk about navigating disruptions in your immigration process, it's important to be as specific as possible. People often confuse many of the terms below, and it leads to a lot of unnecessary consternation. Imagine thinking your entire green card was denied, but it was only rejected for now because you forgot the $85 fee?

Let's define the major types of process disruptions before we go further:

- **Rejection** is often not as bad as it sounds. Having an application rejected simply means that your payment and documents have not been processed because some key parts of your application were missing. This could be because your filing fee was incorrect, you were missing important documents or another reason. Get an immigration lawyer and try again! If you missed a deadline by a day or two, they might have access to magical legal arguments like *nunc pro tunc*, Latin for "now for then."

- **Requests for Evidence (RFEs)** can be frequent based on the administration and they might not be a big deal at all, so it's important to not read too much into them. It simply indicates that more information is needed to make a decision. An RFE is a written letter (and possible fax) with a deadline usually 60-90 days out. Work with your lawyer to prepare your response. Note: an RFE pauses the Premium Processing clock.

- **Notice of Intent to Deny (NOID)** iss better than a denial. Getting a NOID allows you to formulate a response to address the listed reasons. Remember, if you don't want to respond, you can always withdraw and consider trying again later with new evidence of changed circumstances.

- **Denial** means that a governing body has received and reviewed your application and ultimately decided that you didn't meet the criteria for a given status. You can in many circumstances file a Motion to Reopen or Motion to Reconsider or even appeal. Often you can reapply, but you do have to disclose the prior denial.

- **Overstay** refers to stays beyond the permitted duration of your status, which is typically the last day on your petition. If you're in an F-1 or layoff grace period or you have a timely filed application for a new status, you have likely not overstayed.

- **Out of Status and the 3 Year/10 Year Bar:** If you've been out of status 6 months to 1 year and you leave you can't return for 3 years. If you've been out of status for over a year and you leave you can't come back for 10 years. Waivers to overcome these restrictions are extremely hard to obtain.

- **Violation of Status** means engaging in activities that are not permitted by your status, or failing to do activities that are required by your status. For example, an F-1 university freshman on an F-1 needs to be attending class, and tourists cannot work. Committing immigration fraud and other crimes also violate one's status.

- **Visa Revocation** means your visa is no longer valid and cannot be used to re-enter the U.S. Visas can be revoked or canceled at the State Department or CBP's discretion, but this usually only happens under extreme circumstances, such as someone being convicted of a crime.

In all of these situations, you need an immigration lawyer. Best to work with one from the beginning to put your best foot forward and attempt any of these things from ever happening in the first place!

Layoffs and the 60-Day Grace Period

USCIS allows you to stay in the U.S. for a 60-day grace period if you lose your job while you're in the U.S. in E-1, E-2, E-3, H-1B, H-1B1, L-1, O-1, or TN status.

Layoff Insurance: Concurrent H-1Bs

If you have an H-1B and you would like to protect yourself in the event of a potential layoff, consider obtaining a concurrent H-1B. If you have gone through the H-1B lottery, then with two or more concurrent H-1Bs, you're protected if you are laid off by one of your employers because you're still maintaining status. Therefore, in the event of a layoff you wouldn't enter any 60-day grace period, and you would have options such as amending your remaining H-1B to go full time or looking for additional work at another company or your own startup and obtaining a new concurrent H-1B.

How do you get a concurrent H-1B for this situation? Well, if you have already gone through the H-1B lottery and you receive an offer for a second, part-time job, the second company can sponsor you for an additional H-1B at the same time. This second company could even be your own startup, if structured properly to comply with immigration requirements. The second, concurrent H-1B can be structured for a wide range of hours per week (I've seen as little as 5 hours per week consistently get approved). The wage can be hourly or salary.

Before starting to interview for that part-time job or establishing your startup, consult with an experienced immigration lawyer to review your strategy. Also consult with an employment attorney to review your offer letter as well as any present or contemplated privacy, confidentiality and intellectual property or non-disclosure agreements.

Keep in mind: a concurrent H-1B isn't necessarily for everyone. First, you want to make sure you're not jeopardizing your current full-time role by accepting the second job. Second, if you're thinking of building your startup on a concurrent H-1B, you also want to make sure that you're not compromising any of its intellectual property by potential claims from your current employer.

The concurrent H-1B employer will be aware of your existing H-1B, but your current employer wouldn't necessarily find out about the new concurrent H-1B until you get to the H-1B extension or certain parts of the employment-based green card process.

Laid Off? Buy Time to Find a New Role

You may be able to extend your 60-day time runway up to eight months or more by changing your status to another category such as a visitor (6 months), student (Duration of Status), or dependent spouse (tied to the length of your spouse's work status).

For example, you can apply for a change of status to a B-1 business visitor visa, which will let you engage in certain activities such as business formation and fundraising meetings. In B-1, you will be able to stay for six additional months after your 60-day grace period has concluded, and you can apply for B status in parallel to your job search or preparations for another change of status to O-1A or finding a new employer for an H-1B transfer. After the tech layoffs that began in fall of 2022, USCIS confirmed that you can look for a new job while maintaining B-1 or B-2 status.

New Job? Transfer Your H-1B

If you received an offer from your newly established startup or another company for a parttime or fulltime role, congratulations! You might be eligible for an H-1B transfer. In Chapter 9, we'll go more in depth about H-1B transfers and sponsorship.

If you're looking to transfer your H-1B to another company after a layoff, ensure you keep track of your timing with the grace period. The company must ensure that your change of employer petition is received by USCIS on or before the 60th day since your employment ceased.

Therefore, ask your new company to start the Labor Condition Application (LCA) process as soon as possible — submitting an LCA to the U.S. Department of Labor for approval is the first step in getting your H-1B transferred. USCIS requires a certified LCA alongside your new employer's H-1B petition. The Labor Department usually takes a week or two to process an LCA.

If you were laid off on H-1B and in the grace period without a concurrent petition, you're allowed to start working for the company as soon as USCIS receives your H-1B, which must be on or before the 60th day of your grace period. Even while you're waiting for USCIS to adjudicate your petition, you're allowed to remain in the U.S. Enjoy your extended stay!

Take the Plunge: Change Your Status to O-1A

If you were laid off and you've been on the fence about your startup, consider this an opportunity to go all-in and get that O-1!

Many career professionals and aspiring founders I support are surprised to find out that they already qualify for an O-1A. Refer to Chapter 2 for a refresher on O-1As.

If you're planning to pursue an O-1A, start gathering letters of recommendation and evidence that you meet at least three of the eight O-1A requirements. While you're working with an immigration lawyer on your plan (and your backup plan), make sure you assemble all the documents you will need to change your existing status to a new one.

Loss of Status

There are many reasons why you fall out of your immigration status, and all of them are stressful. Perhaps you were denied for a change of status, or you or your company violated your status. Perhaps your visa was dependent on your spouse and you went through a divorce, or you got laid off on a work visa.

Even though you might have accepted some level of risk to change your life and get to the U.S. in the first place, in any of these situations, you might be experiencing a heightened level of anxiety.

Take a deep breath.

You have many paths for moving forward.

Visa Violations

The U.S. immigration system is complicated, to say the least. It's possible to violate your visa accidentally by missing a deadline, failing to take enough classes in school, or working without authorization. You have to be extra careful when you're an immigrant. That's one of the many reasons I always recommend working with an immigration lawyer from start to finish.

Aside from violating your visa or violating the law, you also need to be careful to avoid doing things that a immigration law might consider to be outside the bounds of "good moral character" which is a requirement for eventual citizenship. Ultimately, it's up to the USCIS officer who is evaluating your case to make a determination on whether or not your case represents "good moral character."

Keep in mind that certain medical and recreational and drug use is still illegal at the federal level. For example, even though marijuana for many uses is legal in many states, it's still a controlled substance as of 2023. So for example, an immigrant in California who uses marijuana and doesn't get caught has still committed an offense that would be grounds for removal (aka deportation). If you're an immigrant, "Just Say No."

If you believe that you have violated your visa or have anything on your record that may otherwise influence your immigration status, it's best to proceed with caution and work with an expert immigration attorney. If you have been accused of a crime, avail yourself of a criminal defense attorney that knows immigration ("crimmigration") or partners with an experienced immigration attorney.

Your attorneys will advise you on the best way to proceed, including the consequences of the situation and how to navigate them in your immigration journey. If you can qualify for additional immigration options, they can help you clearly disclose any necessary information truthfully while putting your best foot forward. Remember that lying on your visa paperwork or during an interview is grounds for denial, removal (deportation), or having your existing status revoked — and ignorance of the law is no excuse.

Here's a cautionary tale about staying in your lane. I met an international student who came to me with the following story: Google owns a lot of land in Mountain View, where it was headquartered. It provides free brightly-painted bicycles for use "on campus." The international student was in a neighboring city, several miles from Google, but was planning on going there to meet a friend for lunch. He noticed a Google bike laying on the street and decided to help Google out by attempting to return it to Google HQ while getting to their destination: a win-win.

But before he made it to Google, he was stopped by the city's police, who didn't see things that way and issued a citation for bicycle theft, jeopardizing the international student's immigration status. Thankfully, his immigration and criminal attorneys were able to work together to negotiate a deal with the prosecutor.

Moral of the story: if you are an immigrant, be careful and always avail yourself of good legal counsel.

Immigration Scams

I'll list out a few common immigration scams that I've come across in hopes that you'll be better able to identify them if they come your way.

Often, callers will pose as USCIS and scam people out of money. These calls will appear to come from Washington, D.C. or from a toll-free USCIS number. People report callers threatening them with deportation, or telling them that they'll be put on the Terrorist Watchlist if they don't send a payment through Western Union. Even some people who have had green cards for years have received these calls.

Remember, never send any payment or give any personal information to anyone over the phone. USCIS officials will never ask you for payment, passport, social security numbers, or other personal information over the phone. USCIS will also never contact you through social media accounts like Facebook, Twitter, LinkedIn, etc.

If you receive a call like this, hang up immediately and report the incident to your immigration attorney or to your local USCIS field office.

Those in Spanish-speaking communities in the U.S. should beware of notario fraud. In many Latin American countries, a notario público is qualified to offer legal advice or services. However, this title is not recognized in the U.S. Many people working in the immigration field call themselves notarios and engage in the unauthorized practice of law or file fraudulent immigration applications. One common example is filing a false asylum application to help somebody get a work permit in the short term — the immigrants in these situations usually end up in immigration court as they never actually applied for asylum. These false filings can result in missed deadlines, incorrect forms, false claims, or even deportation.

Beware of companies that offer you an unsolicited job from overseas. If you receive a suspicious job offer by email before you leave your country to come to the U.S., it could be a scam, especially if you're asked to pay money in order to receive your job offer.

Another common scam involves scammers reaching out to you and saying that you've won the Diversity Visa lottery, even if you've never entered, and then asking for personal information or payment to process your application. Report any emails like this to the Federal Trade Commission; the only place to find out if you've been selected for the Diversity Visa lottery is directly on the State Department's DV website.

"Benching" describes a situation where an employer fails to pay an H-1B worker despite not having officially terminated him or her. This can occur if a company is slowing down operations or seeking to cut corners, or if a staffing company doesn't have enough Statements of Work lined up with their clients. "Benching" H-1B employees is illegal; H-1B employees must be paid the minimum prevailing wage as long as they are on H-1B status.

There are also many cases of H-1B employer abuses, such as wage theft or mistreatment. H-1B workers may feel vulnerable and can be afraid to report their employers for violations. However, H-1B whistleblowers are protected and employers are legally prohibited from retaliating against H-1B workers. You can submit an anonymous tip through the Securities and Exchange Commission (SEC) website, which is authorized to provide monetary awards for information that leads to SEC enforcement action.

There are also "extraordinary circumstance" protections for H-1B workers who report fraud or abuse that can grant them eligibility to extend or change their status when they would not normally be able to.

The USCIS website has a list of common scams that you can make yourself familiar with to best protect yourself and your loved ones from fraudsters. This list includes human trafficking, which is a global crime that exploits people for profit.

Human traffickers prey on people who are seeking employment, looking to make money, or are otherwise hoping for a better life. They may promise high-paying jobs or new and exciting opportunities and then coerce victims into labor or services. An employer may ask to see your passport or visa, but do not let them keep it — send a photocopy when possible, just to be safe. No U.S. employer should ever keep your passport while you are working for them. You have the right to hold your own immigration documents after your employer has completed their I-9 inspection.

I once worked with a man who had endured years of human trafficking; he was forced to work on farms across the U.S. until he eventually escaped, and I was able to help him receive a T Visa so he could stay in the U.S. legally. In addition to manual labor industries, human trafficking is also commonly found in the service industry, such as in restaurants and hospitality.

If you have seen or experienced this type of abuse, please call the National Human Trafficking Hotline at 888-373-7888.

Common Immigration Scams

Here are some common immigration scams; head to USCIS to learn more.

- Government impersonators
- Misleading offers of support
- Scams targeting potential participants in Uniting for Ukraine
- Scams targeting the processes for Cubans, Haitians, Nicaraguans, and Venezuelan nationals and their immediate family members
- Human trafficking
- Afghan personal information scam
- Job offer scams
- TPS re-registration scams
- Social media, email offers, and scam websites
- Payments by phone or email
- Winning the visa lottery
- Scams targeting students
- Paying money for connections or jumping the line
- Form I-9 and email scams

If you believe that you've been subject to an immigration scam, reach out to an immigration lawyer to review your options for recourse. You may have options for recourse, such as a designated U visa for crime victims, T visa for human trafficking victims, employment authorization documents (EAD) for H-1B whistleblowers, and visas for domestic violence victims under the Violence Against Women Act (VAWA).

Changes in the Immigration Process

Immigration law changes all the time. Documents change, application fees go up, requirements shift. Sometimes these changes are good — like the potential for a designated startup visa in the future — and sometimes they disrupt the status quo in uncomfortable ways.

With each new U.S. administration, my team and I like to make educated predictions about how the state of immigration will unfold in the coming years.

The Trump administration was hard on immigrants; he issued the Muslim Ban, and many other immigration restrictions including an executive order in 2020 that paused the issuance of H, L, and J visas during the pandemic. While this proclamation was ultimately struck down as an overstep of the president's authority, it still represented a frightening time for people going through the immigration process.

The overall trend so far for the Biden administration has been to improve the operational efficiency of USCIS and the State Department to reduce case processing delays and backlogs. We've also enjoyed a dramatic expansion of the Premium Processing program to include employment-based visas and green cards as well as even F-1 student EAD work permits.

Some hopes for the remainder of this administration include improvements to the International Entrepreneur Parole process as well as the reinterpretation of the employer-employee requirement for H-1B startup founders to enjoy more flexibility in how they structure their companies.

As a founder tasked with pursuing a visa in the U.S., you shouldn't have to take on the additional responsibility of staying up to date on all changes to immigration law that may or may not be relevant to you or your case. My team and I post regular blog posts and podcasts to this end, and my TechCrunch column "Ask Sophie" is reposted on my website for free, so we can make sure you know everything you need to know, when you need to know it.

Case Study: Carlos S.

This case study has been anonymized to protect the identity of those involved.

Carlos S. grew up in Spain. As a kid, he was fascinated by computers and was always programming. After finishing his undergraduate degree in computer science at ESADE in Barcelona and working for a Spanish software company for five years, he decided it was time for him to take a leap and found a startup of his own.

He came to the U.S. on an ESTA for three months. The ESTA program allows citizens of many countries to travel to the U.S. for up to 90 days without a visa. You can read more about ESTA and the Visa Waiver Program (VWP) in Chapter 3.

During his visit to the U.S., Carlos was very proactive. He incorporated his startup, opened a bank account, rented a coworking space, and even raised money from investors that he had been in touch with back in Spain. An impressive feat in 90 days.

But Carlos did not fully understand the constraints of ESTA. He was on a tourist ESTA (WT), not a business ESTA (WB). He stated at the airport that he was coming to be a visitor for pleasure. However, he didn't just see the sights when he was in the U.S. — he took serious steps towards forming his business.

He returned to Spain on time and continued working on his company there while he pursued an E-2 visa based on his personal investment of several hundred thousand dollars into his company. He wanted the E-2 to move to the States, work from his U.S. office, get paid in the U.S., meet with his investors in person; he wanted to be the CEO of his startup in the United States. E-2 visas, covered in Chapter 4, allow founders to enter the U.S. if they have invested a substantial amount of capital to build their business there. It doesn't designate a minimum investment amount, but typically $100,000 is sufficient for many startup business plans.

Carlos had invested far more than $100,000 in his startup's U.S. presence, so he thought the E-2 would be a breeze. But then he got denied, and it was painful.

He came to me for the first time, years later, struggling to find a way to come to the U.S. because his investors were demanding he meet with them.

Why the denial? It turned out that even though he qualified for an E-2 visa and would have been a natural fit, he was denied on the basis of fraud. To prove that he had invested significant funds in starting his U.S. office, his receipts demonstrated that he had incorporated and entered into the lease during his time as an ESTA tourist, when he said that he was only visiting for pleasure.

Committing immigration fraud is a crime, and it stays on your immigration record even if you weren't convicted in a criminal court. There is no easy fix for a situation like this. But Carlos felt pressure from his investors who wanted to meet with him in person more often. He didn't want to tell them that he was experiencing significant hiccups in his visa process; he wanted to reassure them that everything was going smoothly.

When Carlos called, he wanted to understand the consequences of what he was desperately considering: impersonating a U.S. citizen to get into the country. I warned him against this plan and explained that a false claim to U.S. citizenship brings with it a lifetime ban from entering the country. And there is no waiver. I never heard from Carlos S. after that meeting. I hope he stayed outside the United States and found another way to please his investors.

Immigration lawyers may not always give you the answer you're looking for, but they will always be honest with you, and have your best interests at heart. They can help you protect against disruptions and support you to navigate them if they do occur.

Considerations for Naturalization

You've resided lawfully in the U.S. for years while working on your startup and you now qualify to apply for citizenship (also known as naturalization). But, let's take a step back. Should you?

Some of the most common reasons to become a U.S. citizen:

- You want to sponsor family members for green cards, such as your parents or a potential spouse.
- You want to be able to vote.
- You want to be able to leave the U.S. for long periods of time and retain your ability to travel in and out for the long-term.

It's counterintuitive that, after putting in all this work, you wouldn't pursue your U.S. citizenship, but there are a lot of reasons why founders may choose to stay on a green card, or even give up their green cards, as they build their business in the U.S. While these reasons vary from one person to the next, the most common reason is about the money: taxes.

U.S. tax laws are as complicated as its immigration laws. As a citizen, you may have to report your foreign-held assets to the IRS, with serious penalties for not doing so. Unless your home country has specific treaties with the U.S. to this effect, you may also have to pay "double" the taxes, both in the U.S. and your home country. U.S. citizens and green card holders are taxed regardless of where in the world they currently reside, so if you don't see yourself staying in the U.S. for the foreseeable future, you may not want to pursue a green card or citizenship.

As a result of the U.S.'s complicated tax implications, some international banks don't want to do business with U.S. citizens at all, which can be frustrating if you someday live in another country and want to take advantage of the financial services near you.

And let's say your startup is a massive success and it's time to go public. If you're not a citizen or green card holder, you are only subject to the capital gains tax in your home country, which may be lower. Many high-profile founders have given up their U.S. citizenship or green cards in advance of an IPO. I am not a tax advisor and this is something you would need to speak with a cross-border CPA about as far in advance as possible so you can get thorough advice and properly plan ahead.

Some people also choose not to pursue citizenship, or to give up their citizenship, for personal, religious, or political reasons, such as opposing a country's actions abroad or objecting to its political leadership. Note that atheists can opt to remove the word "God" from their Oath of Citizenship if they prefer.

Others may be wary of the "good moral character" requirement for naturalization.

Although the choice is ultimately in your hands, giving up your green card or even citizenship can still represent a major disruption and should be approached with caution and sound legal advice. Your team of experienced immigration lawyers and global mobility tax CPAs can help you decide if these routes make sense for you.

Putting It All Together

The legal landscape may very well change while you're going through the immigration process. My hope is that this chapter gives you some peace of mind that, whatever the case may be, you'll be able to weather those changes. We covered some options on what you can do if you lose your visa status, and went over a few of my best practices for navigating disruptions in the immigration process.

Learn more and get support when you need it.

May it Simply Fall Away

This has been a personal prayer of mine for some time:

Whatever is no longer needed, may it simply fall away.

So much of what we experience can be released.

The hard times, the sticky bits we've been holding on to, or that have held onto us.

Let's learn from them, and then release them.

This learning isn't easy. It's often very painful. I wish we could all learn whatever it is we need to learn in this life through joy and love and attraction, but as the Rolling Stones so aptly put it, "You can't always get what you want / But if you try sometimes, well, you might find / You get what you need."

If you want to super-charge your personal growth, there's no way out but through.

With money, when you die, you can't take it with you. The same is true for all of our uncertainties, stressors, and trauma. So why hold on to them so tightly?

CHAPTER 9

Build Your Team of Top Global Talent

Congratulations on making it to our last chapter! We've covered so much in our journey. This last chapter before I send you on your way is a primer on how to hire international talent once you've established yourself and your startup in the United States.

We'll cover all of your options, from sponsoring someone for an H-1B, to all the different visas you can use to bring talent here, to transferring an existing H-1B and protecting your company along the way. Although you aren't required to offer immigration sponsorship to current or future employees, you may not discriminate based on national origin.

That being said, when you're interviewing candidates, it's permissible to ask whether they require immigration sponsorship. If a candidate says yes, you can find out details to inform your immigration plan, such as:

- Which country were you born in?
- What is your current immigration status?
- When did that status start?
- When does your status expire?
- Have you started any stages of the green card process?
- Have you had any immigration issues?
- Do any of your immediate family members need to be included in your immigration process?

Ready to learn more? Here we go.

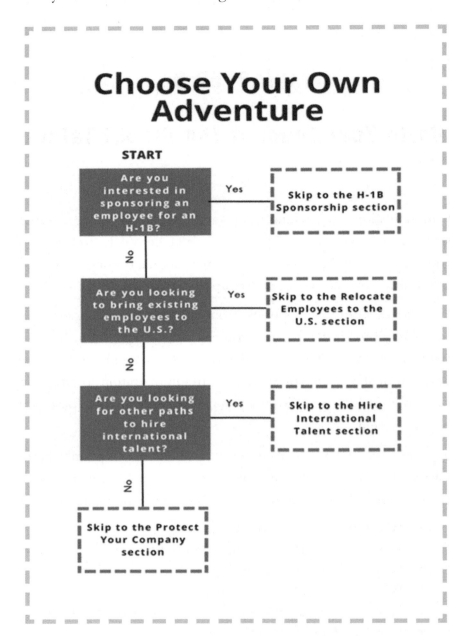

H-1B Sponsorship

People are your biggest asset. As you grow your company with top global talent, thank you for deciding to provide immigration peace of mind to your team through H-1B sponsorship!

Thinking globally when it comes to hiring is a great way to not only open up your recruiting pipeline but also bring diversity of thought and experience to your company, which allows innovation to flourish.

As always, I highly recommend working with an experienced startup immigration attorney to support this process, particularly since USCIS tends to scrutinize early-stage companies. An attorney can help you navigate the process, avoid missteps, and submit a strong visa application on behalf of your employees while staying within your budget — and possibly even saving you time and money in the long run, which can help you preserve your startup's runway.

It's never too early to start assembling the documents you will need to submit to sponsor someone for an H-1B. Your startup will need to be incorporated, have a mailing and physical address, get its tax ID number from the I.R.S., and have a bank account with funds to prove that it is capable of sponsorship. You will need the incorporation and FEIN tax ID number in order to submit a Labor Condition Application (LCA).

How to Establish Your Company for Immigration Sponsorship

You may decide to set up your company in a way that allows it to sponsor visas and green cards, while also attracting funding from investors. Here are some best practices:

- Consider incorporating your company as a Delaware Corp with C-Corp tax status, which is most common in Silicon Valley.

- If you need an H-1B transfer as a founder, set up an employer-employee relationship between yourself and your startup. This typically means that someone else at your startup, such as your Board of Directors, must supervise you and have the ability to fire you. USCIS guidance on this is in flux and things might get easier for founders, so talk to an immigration lawyer about this to evaluate the ownership and control of your startup and the employer-employee relationship.

- Fully establish your company legally and have at least a couple of months of records of compliance such as:
  - Articles of Incorporation
  - State Certificate of Registration
  - Company bylaws
  - Partnership agreements
  - And any other relevant legal formation documents

- Obtain a federal Employer Identification Number (EIN) from the IRS and keep the IRS SS-4 letter assigning your company's EIN as evidence.

- Set up a U.S. bank account, deposit some initial funding, and keep your statements.

- Set up your branding and web presence including logo and letterhead, website, one-pager PDFs and other marketing materials, and a pitch deck explaining your business.

- Talk to your immigration lawyer about how much of a physical office or coworking space you'll need depending on the visa type and make sure you have a reliable mailing address to receive snail mail correspondence from government agencies.
- Save evidence of your company's funding and operations
  - Funding documentation
  - Wire transfers
  - Cap tables
  - Term sheets
  - Contracts
  - Letters of intent
  - Employment records
  - Records of payments to contractors
  - Org chart

What You Need For an H-1B Petition

To sponsor an employee's H-1B visa, you will need:

- A job description for your beneficiary (the individual your startup is sponsoring) and the minimum requirements for the position
- A job offer letter to the beneficiary, including job title, detailed duties, benefits, salary, and start date. October is the start of the federal fiscal year, so if your beneficiary is selected for a given year's lottery, that's the earliest their start date can be if you're seeking a brand new H-1B (it can be any time of year for a transfer)
- Your company's articles of incorporation, term sheet, and cap tables if your startup formed recently
- Your company's bank statements, tax returns, and other financial documents that show your company can pay the prevailing wage for the beneficiary's position and location
- Marketing materials, company reports, pitch decks, business plans, and screenshots of the company website that show that your startup is actively operating

For the sponsorship process, your H-1B candidate will need a current resume, any diplomas, certificates, and transcripts, current and past immigration documents, and certified translations of any documents that are not in English.

Keep in mind that there is typically a six-year maximum stay with an H-1B visa — usually a three-year period with one three-year extension — and many companies retain talented team members beyond this timeframe by beginning the green card sponsorship process after succeeding on with the initial H-1B.

If your employees are from countries like India and China with high levels of immigration, they can receive some peace of mind through the American Competitiveness in the 21st Century Act (AC21) which enabled H-1B holders to extend their visa beyond the six-year maximum if a year or more has passed since they filed their application for labor certification or I-140 immigrant petition and they have not yet heard back. AC21 also makes it easier for H-1B holders to switch jobs without losing their place in the green card line if their green card adjustment application has been pending for at least 180 days.

A note: if your candidate or new hire has decided to pursue a marriage-based green card on their own and you would have otherwise sponsored their employment-based green card, your company should consider paying. Many startups do this. Marriage-based green cards take about one-third of the time and one-third of the money compared to employment-based green cards, and are not subject to annual quotas. If handled correctly, this could be a win-win for both your valued team member and your startup.

H-1B Lottery

Your startup can register your employees for the H-1B lottery — as of 2023, it only costs ten dollars to do so, though this number is likely to increase to a few hundred dollars. But make sure to only register your employee once, or else they will be automatically disqualified.

The number of H-1B visas issued each year to for-profit companies is capped at 85,000. Colleges, universities, nonprofits affiliated with colleges or universities, nonprofit research organizations, and government research organizations are exempt from the H-1B cap and lottery process. If your candidate has only worked for a cap-exempt employer, their H-1B visa cannot be transferred to your company, but the individual might be eligible for concurrent employment at your startup in addition to that other position, without going through the lottery.

If you don't already have a USCIS account, you will have to make one as a "registrant" (sponsoring company). The USCIS website has many helpful videos and guides on how to navigate this process. The odds of being selected for the H-1B lottery vary by year and depend on the number of petitions.

Usually, the lottery is open during March and winners are notified in April. You will then have until the end of June to submit your H-1B petition to USCIS. Sometimes there are additional lottery rounds if not all 85,000 visas are used.

If your employees are selected in the lottery, your startup can then prepare, submit, and pay the required fees to USCIS for an H-1B filing. I recommend paying for Premium Processing for your H-1B petition depending on the beneficiary's start date and when his or her current immigration status expires. With Premium Processing, you'll hear back within 15 days of submitting your petition, with the added benefit that your attorney will get email updates from USCIS as well.

Some people fear that Premium Processing leads to a higher risk of receiving a request for evidence (RFE) or denial, which I can officially debunk. In fact, Premium Processing ensures better communication with USCIS, which is valuable if you're filing a complex H-1B case.

Cap-Exempt H-1B Petition

Some employers, like institutions of higher education, non-profits related to institutions of higher education, non-profit research organizations, and government research organizations, are considered "cap-exempt," which means they are not subject to the H-1B lottery.

One example of a cap-exempt company is Open Avenues, which hires international professionals to teach university students in the U.S. If a candidate is on a cap-exempt H-1B visa with a program like Open Avenues, your startup can sponsor them for a concurrent H-1B, without the limited timing or randomness of the H-1B lottery.

Transfer an H-1B to Your Company

Bringing someone to your company who is already in a nonimmigrant status at another U.S. company will enable you and your prospective hire to avoid having to go through the annual H-1B lottery process.

Here are the questions I usually get when a startup is considering hiring someone who is already on an H-1B:

- What questions should we ask job candidates?
- How risky is the process of transferring an H-1B to a new employer?
- How quickly can an H-1B transferee start working for us?

In terms of risk, an H-1B transfer is pretty predictable if your startup can pay the candidate's salary and you're offering a professional role. It's definitely less risky than a new H-1B because you do not have to go through the lottery process again.

Although a candidate currently on an H-1B might technically be able to start working when your company receives a receipt from USCIS for the pending petition, most companies and candidates usually want to play it safe. It's possible to work with your legal team to craft the candidate's start date for the future so that they will find out if the transfer has been approved before being required to start. This would also give them more time to give notice to their current company. This could minimize their immigration risk and it demonstrates that you care about your team.

To transfer someone who is on an H-1B to your company, you will still need to go through the regular H-1B petition process, which means you'll have to submit a Labor Condition Application (LCA) to the U.S. Department of Labor for approval before you send your petition to USCIS.

Because of the complexities of the H-1B transfer and extension process and timing as well as the high stakes, I recommend that companies — particularly early-stage startups — work with an experienced immigration attorney, even before extending the offer to your candidate.

Keep in mind that, if you transfer an employee's H-1B to your company from another company, the clock on their six-year maximum does not reset.

What You Need For an H-1B Transfer

To transfer an employee's H-1B visa to your startup, you will to demonstrate:

- An offer letter containing their job title and salary
- A detailed description of their responsibilities and duties
- Evidence that your startup is a real company, such as a company brochure or screenshots of your website, marketing materials, pitch decks, etc.
- Proof that your startup can pay the prevailing wage

Your prospective employee will usually be required to show:

- Valid passport with their H-1B visa stamp
- I-797 approval notice
- I-94 arrival/departure form with an unexpired departure date
- Resume or CV
- Any diplomas or certificates
- University transcripts

Prevailing Wages for an H-1B

I've used the term "prevailing wage" a few times in this chapter. Let's talk about that a bit more.

The prevailing wage requirement is primarily there to protect H-1B workers from exploitation for cheap labor and it also serves to protect U.S. workers from unfair wage competition. Prevailing wages rates are reviewed and updated every year to ensure they keep up with economic changes such as inflation and labor trends, and is the average salary paid to similarly qualified workers in similar positions in the same geographic area. The prevailing wage is a minimum — employers can pay more, but not less.

There are four prevailing wage levels based on different levels of responsibility and experience. See the table below for reference as of 2022:

Wage Level	Salary Percentile*	Approximate Prevailing Wage Range	Description
1	17th	$38,000 - $51,000	Entry-level
2	34th	$51,000 - $65,000	Qualified
3	50th	$65,000 - $75,000	Experienced
4	67th	$78,000 - $90,000	Fully competent

*Salary percentile is the inclusive range within which an employee's salary falls. For example, an H-1B employee with Level 4 wages will make more than 67% of employees with their qualifications in their geographic area.

As an employer, make sure you maintain paying your employee at the prevailing wage from the time of filing throughout the duration of their approved status.

H-1B Amendments

According to USCIS regulations, employers have to file an amended H-1B petition whenever there is a 'material' change in an employee's work conditions or details. These changes may include:

- Change in work location outside of the commuting area of original worksite(s)
- Change in job title
- Significant change in job duties (e.g. core duties, role changes to manager, etc.)
- Reduction in salary
- Change in work hours (part-time to full-time or vice versa)
- Other changes

Working from home instead of from an office may qualify as a change in work location if the employee's home is in a different metropolitan area than their office, or if they work fifty miles or more away from their original work location stated on the petition.

Promotions may require H-1B amendments if the employee's job duties have significantly changed. For example, if your employee is promoted from a software engineer to a senior software engineer with similar core duties, you would likely not need to file an amendment. But if they are promoted from a software engineer to a technical project manager, you may need to do so.

An amendment can get rejected if the changes no longer qualify the H-1B recipient for the visa. A rejection does not invalidate an existing approved H-1B petition, but it's still worth working with an experienced immigration attorney to make sure your amendment is filled out thoroughly and correctly. USCIS usually takes 100-150 days to process H-1B amendment petitions if you choose not to opt for Premium Processing, currently at $2,500 per petition.

H-1B Extensions

H-1Bs are only granted in increments up to 3 years, so you will have to apply for H-1B extensions for your employees down the line to use up their 6-year maximum. Employees are eligible for H-1B extensions if they are currently in valid H-1B status and they will remain employed in a speciality occupation moving forward.

Luckily, you don't have to worry about H-1B caps and the lottery for a renewal. To get an extension, you will have to file another Petition for a Nonimmigrant Worker and submit additional filing fees. Employees with a pending H-1B renewal are able to continue work for their current employer for up to 240 days or until their renewal is approved. Similarly, if you have filed a PERM or an Immigrant Petition for Alien Worker (I-140) for the employee and those petitions have been pending for more than a year, the H-1B can be extended beyond the six year maximum.

If your employee departs the U.S. while their H-1B extension is pending, they will most likely have to wait outside the U.S. for the extension to be approved. Caveats like this make it even more important to work with an immigration lawyer.

H-1B Recapture

H-1Bs are generally granted in three-year increments for a total of six years, but this period can be extended in certain circumstances. H-1B recapture refers to a process where you can "recapture" days in which the employee was outside the U.S. in order to make sure that you utilize every day of the six year maximum. The six-year maximum is cumulative, not consecutive, and any trip outside of the U.S. for longer than a day can be recaptured.

For example, if your H-1B employee took a two-week vacation every year during their six years on an H-1B, they can technically recapture three months of time. These three months can make a huge difference as you navigate extensions and any necessary changes of status.

But recapture is not automatic: USCIS doesn't keep track of your employee's departures from, and arrivals to, the U.S. You as the employer can request the time abroad to be recaptured on your employee's behalf at any time while their H-1B is still active through a petition for extension. Additionally, if you held H-1B status 8 years ago for 2 years, you could apply for the "remaining time." There is no limit in terms of how long ago you held the original H-1B status.

H-1B recapture doesn't require reasons for why the employee traveled abroad, just proof of the exit and return in the form of passport stamps, Form I-94 arrival or departure records, and/or plain tickets.

USCIS may grant all, part, or none of the requested recapture time, and does not typically send an RFE for trips that are missing evidence, so make sure to do your due diligence and ask your employees to maintain and provide thorough records.

Transfer Employees to Your U.S. Office with the L-1

Let's say you built your business abroad and you want to move yourself and your employees to the U.S., or your remote contractors abroad want to move to the U.S. and work with you in-person.

Consider your options to make this a reality. I suggest you begin by setting up a legal entity of your company in the country where the employees in question work today. Talk to your immigration and corporate attorneys to determine the right type of entity (such as a corporation or limited liability company) and the right type of relationship (such as parent, subsidiary, branch or affiliate).

We spoke about L-1 visas a bit in Chapter 4; they can be a strong route to bring your professionals to the U.S. if your company has another office abroad. L-1s can be issued for workers performing managerial or executive duties, or employees with specific expertise of a company's goods, services, and management practices. L-1As are for managerial or executive positions, while L-1Bs are specifically for specialized knowledge workers.

There are several benefits to the L-1 visa. They allow employees to bring their families to the U.S. and allow their spouses to work. There is no minimum education level for employees to qualify for an L-1. They can also be applied to year-round with no cap or lottery required.

On the other hand, they come with intense company requirements, and you need a physical U.S. office. Your startup must do business in the U.S., which refers to the regular provisioning of goods and or services, not merely retaining employees.

Qualifications for an L-1A

Employees must demonstrate the following to qualify for an L-1A visa:

- Have been working on the payroll for the employer abroad for one continuous year within the past three years.

- Have an executive or managerial position in the U.S. with the same employer that has broad discretion to make decisions with little oversight, supervisory duties, or manages a key function.

Qualifications for an L-1B

Employees must demonstrate the following to qualify for an L-1B visa:

- Have been working on the payroll for the employer abroad for one continuous year within the past three years.

- Have a position with the employer or one of its affiliates in the U.S. that requires advanced, specialized knowledge or expertise of the organization's products, services, processes or procedures.

L-1s are initially valid for three years, and they can be extended every two years after that initial period for seven years in total for an L-1A and five years in total for an L-1B.

The L-1 is a dual-intent visa, which means it's fine to simultaneously pursue Permanent Residence while working in the U.S. If you want your employees to stay longer, the L-1A visa offers a path to an EB-1C green card for multinational managers and executives. The L-1B visa offers a path to either an EB-2 or EB-3 green card.

Hire International Talent

The severe U.S. tech talent shortage is prompting professionals to negotiate better compensation packages, and companies increasingly leverage visa and green card sponsorship as a benefit to attract and retain international talent.

Before we dive into visa specifics, please be aware that I recommend you consult an experienced immigration attorney who can help you devise an immigration strategy for prospective international hires, as well as provide guidance on what visas would be appropriate given the job opening and prospective candidate.

Okay, let's check out your options!

F-1 OPT and STEM OPT Work Permits

The majority of international talent in the U.S. as students are here on F-1 visas, which we covered in Chapter 2.

In that same chapter, we covered how F-1 students can go on to work for 12-24 months through CPT (Curricular Practical Training), OPT (Optional Practical Training), or STEM OPT extensions after they graduate.

OPT allows for 12 months of employment, and you can add another 24 months on top of that through STEM OPT if your potential employee is in a STEM-related field. Keep in mind that STEM OPT requires a training program approved by the potential employee's DSO (Designated School Official) and your company to be enrolled in the government's E-verify system. Find more on this in Chapter 2.

With OPT and STEM OPT, you can hire F-1 students out of college for a total of up to three years. Their hope is usually that your company will enter them in the H-1B lottery annually during this period. If your international employee is not selected for the lottery during this time, consider a cap-exempt H-1B or an O-1A as a back up option.

O-1A Visa

I would recommend starting with the H-1B lottery process mentioned in this chapter, but if your prospective hire isn't selected, or you need to get them working for you before October, a great option for startup talent is an O-1A extraordinary ability visa. You can read more about O-1As in Chapter 2 and Chapter 4.

More and more of my startup clients are choosing to pursue this route to hire key executives and individual contributors with niche expertise such as scientists and researchers or even startup-specific roles such as growth hackers. While the bar for qualifying for an O-1A is much higher than for an H-1B, the process is much quicker, and the O-1A does not have an annual lottery with which to contend.

Some good news: consular offices can now waive the in-person interview requirement for some individuals seeking nonimmigrant visas like H-1Bs and O-1As. Individuals may have the interview waived if they were previously issued any type of visa, they have never been refused a visa, they have no ineligibility, or they are citizens or nationals of a country that participates in the Visa Waiver Program (VWP). This change happened temporarily during the COVID-19 pandemic and has been recently extended for the short-term.

Country-Specific Visas

Depending on your candidate's country of citizenship, you may have special sponsorship options. For example, specific visas exist for certain countries based on treaties, and there are also special work visas for citizens of Australia, Canada, Chile, Mexico, and Singapore. These statuses are available for candidates currently abroad as well as for individuals transferring from other companies in the U.S.

E-1 or E-2 Visa

The U.S. also has trade treaties with some countries that enable citizens of those countries to get an E-1 or E-2 visa for essential employees in a supervisor or executive position, or those with specialized skills. In order for an international employee to be eligible for an E-1 or E-2, your startup must be majority-owned by individuals or an entity from that same treaty country.

An E-1 visa allows foreign nationals whose home country has a treaty with the U.S. to come to the U.S. to work in international trade on the behalf of your startup. Trade refers to the exchange of goods, services, or technology between the U.S. and the treaty country, and includes:

- Banking
- Insurance
- Transportation
- Tourism
- Communications

E-2 visas allow a foreign national to enter the U.S. based on an investment in a U.S. business. They are also available to non-investor employees, as long as the person is of the same nationality as the founder, and is going to do a job in the U.S. that is executive, managerial, or otherwise specialized.

The current list of E-1 and E-2 Treaty Countries is maintained by the State Department.

You can read more about E-1 and E-2 visas in Chapter 4.

E-3 Visa

If the candidate is Australian, an E-3 visa will allow them to work in the U.S. in a speciality occupation. It has an educational requirement of a Bachelor's degree or equivalent. A maximum of 10,500 E-3 visas are available each year, and the process is similar to an H-1B in that it requires you to file an LCA with the U.S. Department of Labor. But you can apply at any time of year seeking 2 years of stay in the U.S., and the 10,500 cap has never been met, a key advantage over the H-1B category.

H-1B1 Visa

If the candidate is a citizen of Chile or Singapore, they may qualify for an H-1B1 speciality occupation visa, which is an H-1B earmarked for citizens of these two countries. Thanks to special treaties between the U.S., Chile, and Singapore, professionals may qualify for

H-1B1s on a fast-tracked basis. The period of employment is one year with unlimited one-year extensions. Each year, 1,400 H-1B1 visas are reserved for Chileans and another 5,400 are reserved for Singaporeans — these visa caps are rarely met.

TN Visa

Professionals from Canada and Mexico can work for you on TN visas. TN stands for "Treaty National" and originally referred to the North American Free Trade Alliance (NAFTA) Treaty between Canada, the United States, and Mexico which President Clinton signed back in the 90's. In 2020, the United States-Mexico-Canada Agreement (USCMA) replaced NAFTA as the basis for this visa; the criteria for qualification did not change.

TN visas are limited to professions listed in treaty agreements, but most of those jobs overlap with H-1B speciality occupations. This visa happens to be difficult to use for CEOs because of its very strict requirements against self-employment, but can easily be used for CTOs or other key positions.

J-1 Visas

The J-1 visa is an educational and cultural exchange visa available to foreign nationals who participate in an approved program for teaching, lecturing, studying, conducting research, consulting, or receiving training or medical education. The purpose of the J-1 is to promote knowledge and cultural exchange between the U.S. and other countries for work and education. It's an attractive option for both participants and employers as there is no cap or lottery for this type of visa.

J is a nonimmigrant status and it can be challenging to get another work visa or green card after participating in some J-1 programs.

The three types of J-1 recipients that startups typically hire are:

- **J-1 Researchers:** Candidates must have a minimum of a bachelor's degree and a full-time academic position. J-1 research scholars can stay in the U.S. for a maximum of five years.

- **J-1 Trainees:** Candidates must have either a degree or professional certificate and at least one year of work experience outside the U.S., or at least five years of work experience outside the U.S. On a J-1, they can't work in an unskilled position or one that requires 20% or more of clerical or office support work. J-1 trainees can stay in the U.S. for a maximum of 18 months.

- **J-1 Interns:** Candidates must be enrolled at a college or university outside the U.S. or have graduated from one in the last 12 months. The maximum stay for J-1 interns is one year.

At the end of an employee's J-1, they may be able to participate in another J-1 program or apply for a different visa.

Employees to the 212(e) two-year foreign residence requirement must return to their home country for at least two years when their visa expires before they can get certain visas such as H-1Bs or a green card. In some cases, they can get a waiver.

Also keep in mind that these two years don't have to be consecutive. You can add separate trips together, with no expiration date, to meet your two-year requirement so you can make progress towards receiving a green card while fulfilling your requirement at the same time.

However, there is no requirement to get the 212(e) 2-year foreign residence requirement waived before obtaining an O-1A visa for extraordinary ability!

Case Study: Daryna R.

This case study has been anonymized to protect the identity of those involved.

Daryna R. grew up in a small town in western Ukraine. She loved her home country and has fond memories of spending time with friends and hiking with her family in the mountains. She received both her undergraduate and master's degree from Lviv Polytechnic National University where she studied applied linguistics. But she wanted to try living abroad for a while, so she pursued a second master's degree at Macalester College in Saint Paul, Minnesota on an F-1 student visa.

Upon graduating from her masters program, she wasn't ready to go back. She wanted to stay in the Minneapolis area and revisit her original love: applied linguistics. She got a job at a local AI company that specialized in natural language processing and would sponsor her H-1B visa.

In early 2022, however, Russia invaded Ukraine, and Daryna worried about her family. She wasn't able to visit them, and was fearful of losing her job and therefore her visa as layoffs proliferated in the tech world throughout the year.

Questions burned through her mind: Should she look for a second job so she could have a concurrent H-1B? Would she be able to apply for asylum if she lost her job?

And if she wasn't laid off, would she potentially be able to bring her family over to the U.S.?

Daryna was also four years into her H-1B's 6-year limit. She was weighed down by anxiety, but multiple things made her feel blessed in the months that followed.

Number one: she survived two rounds of layoffs, and her employer expressed sincere interest in making sure her H-1B status was protected. Her employer communicated with her in advance that her job was safe, and let her take advantage of their in-house counsel if she had any questions or needed support.

Number two: she was selected for the Diversity Lottery her first time ever entering. After four years on an F-1 and another four on an H-1B, Daryna finally got her green card. Her status was no longer dependent on an employer — the weight that had been on her shoulder for months lifted.

After five years of permanent residence, she intends to become a citizen so she can petition for her parents as immediate relatives as well as start the process for her siblings's green cards.

She thinks about her family every day, but feels nothing but joy about her time in the U.S. and her new Permanent Residence. It makes her proud that she can support her family, and she's grateful for her employer for taking a chance and sponsoring her H-1B to begin with, as well as providing additional support and reassurance during times of uncertainty.

Protect Your Company

You've heard my refrain over and over throughout this book, but I'll keep saying it: it's best to work with a specialized immigration attorney and other legal and tax experts when navigating the immigration process for yourself and your employees.

With the rise of remote work, consider the tax implications of a distributed workforce. Corporate, employment, and privacy laws also differ in each state of the U.S., as well as in each country where your international employees might be living. The right attorney can help guide in creating a distributed work policy for your company so you can avoid penalties, lawsuits, and fines.

There are other intricacies, too. For example, if you are sponsoring someone's H-1B and they are terminated from their role, you have to notify USCIS and cover the reasonable cost of their return ticket home. Your immigration attorney can support you with navigating these nuances. They can also assist you in supporting laid off workers on visas with consultations about navigating their next steps. They can offer you tips on how to best care for these employees such as swapping out a severance payment for a longer end-date of employment to allow more time for the job search.

The ultimate goal here is to protect your company. We are here to help you do just that.

Putting It All Together

There are many different routes and considerations when bringing in international talent to your startup. Are they already in the U.S., or are you bringing them in from abroad? Are they already on a visa, or are you helping them through the process? Do they already work for you, or are you looking to hire them now?

For now, let's take a look at all of the visa options I typically recommend for hiring international talent:

Status	Approximate Processing Time*	Premium Processing Available	Length of Stay	Annual Cap
E-1	2-4 weeks	Yes	2 years, with 2-year extensions, typically visa valid for 5 years	No cap
E-2	2-8 months	Yes	2 years, with 2-year extensions, typically visa valid for 5 years	No cap
E-3	2-4 weeks	Yes	1 year, with two 1-year extensions	10,500
H-1B	6-8 months	Yes	Up to 3 years at a time, typically up to 6 years total unless green card sponsored	85,000
Cap-Exempt H-1B	6-8 months	Yes	Up to 3 years at a time, typically up to 6 years total unless green card sponsored	No cap
H1-B1	6-8 months	Yes	1 year, with two 1-year extensions	1,400 for Chile and 5,400 for Singapore
J-1	2-3 months	No	12-18 months for trainee, up to 5 years for researcher	No cap
L-1A	6-12 months	Yes	3 years followed by 2 year extensions for up to 7 years total	No cap
L-1B	6-8 months	Yes	3 years followed by 2 year extensions for up to 5 years total	No cap
O-1A	1-2 months	Yes	3 years, with 1-year extensions	No cap
TN	2-6 months with USCIS 2-4 weeks at border	Yes	3 years, with unlimited 3-year extensions	No cap

*Without Premium Processing

The different sections in this chapter will help you get organized, no matter the situation.

Recruit and retain the world's best and brightest. My team is here to help!

Heart-Centered Leadership

Jamais Cascio, a futurist and distinguished fellow at the Institute for the Future in Palo Alto chatted on my podcast about how the world today can feel brittle, anxious, non-linear, and incomprehensible — an acronym he famously dubbed, "BANI."

Cascio shared three mindsets for heart-centered leadership:

1. **Resilience:** Resilience means being able to withstand a shock to the system without breaking. Lean companies, those who keep themselves small and reactive, who hide their hearts away, are more prone to breaking. Building in slack in the form of talented hires and additional resources can affect profit but offers that built-in resilience. More people to care for one another.

2. **Improvisation:** Remain creative and nimble and be ready to embrace change. Open your heart to possibilities — both professional and personal.

3. **Empathy:** Probably the most critical of the three, empathy involves recognizing the humanity in others. It involves knowing that what we do matters to others now and in the future.

Embrace these mindsets of resilience, improv and empathy while developing your immigration strategy. Practice heart-centered leadership and offer stability to your international talent.

In turn, you'll retain the best people, foster innovation and build longevity for your startup.

The role of the heart is critical in business success.

CHAPTER 10

You're Ready!

We usually end our chapters together on a note of wisdom, but seeing as this is the end of the book, the end of the road for us together today, I'd like to think out loud with you for a little while.

My dad often told me as a little girl that courage and bravery aren't the same thing.

Bravery is full of bravado: brash and fueled by adrenaline.

But courage -- courage is doing the right thing, even when you're scared.

The word courage shares a root with the French word cœur, meaning the "heart."

Courage is doing the right thing, even when you're scared.

When you have two equal honest and forthright paths, how do you know which one is right?

You have to dig deep into what your heart wants, and figure out what's right for you.

Sometimes there's a seeming conflict and attempting to embrace duality breaks our hearts, or breaks our hearts open.

It's as Leonard Cohen said: cracks are where the light gets in.

Or it's like the Japanese Kintsugi pottery, broken and forged back together with gold.

It's scary to put everything on the line and chase your dreams.
But that's what courage is all about.

I believe in you, dear reader. I can't wait to meet you, and I'm already proud we are connected.

Have courage.

On Advocacy

I hope you've enjoyed our time together as much as I have.

One of the biggest challenges in writing this) book was that immigration law changes all the time.

Even now, I'm actively working towards reform in a few areas. If I have to write another version of this book in a few years because those initiatives have been realized, that would be a blessing!

I'm advocating for a number of improvements to the immigration process, including a Startup Visa for founders like you as well as extending the 60-day grace period to 180 days, making F-1 a dual intent status, and allowing STEM PhDs to self-petition for green cards. We want to remove per-country limits on Visa Bulletins and increase the number of employment-sponsored visas and green cards available each year.

Each year, 140,000 employment-based green cards become available, plus any unused green cards from the family-based categories from the previous year. My team and I have long advocated for both increasing the cap on the number of employment-based green cards and eliminating the per-country cap, both of which will require action from Congress to go into effect.

Why? I want to live in a world where every child has the freedom to create, so they can actualize their potential.

I want to empower all the others whose missions are to protect our planet, save lives, and help manifest abundance for all. There are so many ways you can pave the way for others and light up their path.

Thank you for following your heart to do your mission that helps make the world a better place, and thank you for allowing me to be a part of your journey.

Resources for What's Next

My hope in writing this book was that I could reach and help as many people as possible. Ready to take the next step?

Here's how to get started with my law firm, Alcorn Immigration Law:

- Request your free workbook with proof of purchase. This book's workbook contains useful activities and thought-provoking exercises to help you chart your path forward.

- Get a Visa or Green Card with Alcorn Immigration Law. Our legal team is passionate about helping you obtain immigration freedom!

- Subscribe to our newsletter to stay in the know as U.S. immigration laws and regulations update and change.

- Take part in Alcorn Academy: Extraordinary Ability Prep Course. This self-paced course contains 15 modules over eight hours, plus special handouts and extra resources.

- Try out Legal Launch. Are you qualified for O-1A, EB-1A, or EB-2 NIW? If not, we'll tell you what to do to qualify — and if so, we'll credit the course fee to your legal costs to get started on your case.

- Listen to the Immigration Law For Tech Startups Podcast. Twice a month, I bring on the brightest minds in law and immigration to talk about issues and aspirations.

- Read Ask Sophie, my column with TechCrunch, to find answers to the frequently asked questions I get from founders like you.

Enjoy Your Journey!

Made in the USA
Las Vegas, NV
05 November 2023

80314682R00115